# BASIC MANAGEMENT SKILLS

Essential reading for first time managers, supervisors and existing leaders who want to upgrade their skills

Chris Thomas

© 2010 Chris Thomas. All rights reserved.
ISBN 978-0-9564959-0-7

Published by Nicholas Thomas as part of the Managers Toolbox Series.

No part of this book may be reprinted or reproduced, or utilized in any form including by electronic, mechanical or other means, now known or hereafter invented, including photocopying or storing by electronic means without the written permission of the publisher.

# CONTENTS

## Chapter 1
## Introduction — 1

- What is the problem? — 2
- Why change at all? — 3
- Why does change happen? — 4
- Risks and benefits of change — 5
- Typical changes — 6
- Born to lead — 8
- Benefits of becoming a better manager — 8
- Benefits for your family — 9
- Guaranteed to work — 10
- About this book — 10

## Chapter 2
## Role and responsibilities — 13

- Who is a supervisor? — 14
- What is a supervisor? — 15
- What are the resources other than himself? — 16
- Which is the most important resource? — 17
- The four directions — 17
- The management cycle — 18
- Management levels — 21
- Management by walk around — 22
- Task analysis — 23
- Barriers to the effectiveness of the supervisor — 25
- Destroying the barriers — 27

## Chapter 3
## Management by Objectives — 29

- Introduction — 30
- What are SMART objectives? — 31
- How it works — 34
- The performance commitment — 36
- The 80 / 20 principle (Pareto) — 37
- The main benefits of MBO — 39
- Murphy's law — 40

## Chapter 4
## The art of planning — 43

- The concept of planning — 44
- The basic planning process — 46
- Objectives — 46
- Get the facts — 47
- Evaluate alternatives — 48
- Develop the work scope — 51
- Prepare the plan — 52
- Activity lists — 52
- Bar charts — 54
- Dependencies — 58
- Action lists — 60
- Networks — 62

## Chapter 5
## How to get organized     63

- Introduction — 64
- Organizational structure — 65
- Facilities and working environment — 67
- Working within the system — 67
- Sources of additional resources — 69
- Work standards and procedures — 70
- Day to day organization — 70
- Materials management — 72

## Chapter 6
## Control function     75

- Introduction — 76
- The control function in the management cycle — 76
- The people factor — 77
- Setting standards — 78
- Measurement — 79
- Putting it together — 82
- The formal approach — 82
- Control documents — 83
- Action — 84

## Chapter 7
## Time management — 85

- Introduction — 86
- It's your call — 87
- The five stages to success — 87
- Stage 1 - Get organized — 88
- Stage 2 - Analyze how you spend your time — 90
- Stage 3 - Work load planning — 91
- Stage 4 - Create a work load planning system — 92
- Stage 5 - Eliminate notorious time wasters — 95
- Some suggested solutions — 98
- Sustainability — 100

## Chapter 8
## Making decisions — 101

- Introduction — 102
- Dealing with simplistic decisions — 103
- Chose the right management style — 104
- Types of decisions — 105
- The rational decisive making process — 106
- Problem solving techniques — 107
- Attitude — 108

## Chapter 9
## Giving instructions — 109

- Introduction — 110
- Use of authority — 110
- The four key steps — 111
- Don't give orders — 111
- Be clear — 113
- Check list for giving instructions — 114

## Chapter 10
## Assertive behavior — 115

- Introduction — 116
- What makes a winner or loser? — 116
- Don't underestimate your importance — 117
- It's your choice — 118
- Your style — 119
- What is behavior? — 120
- What are passive, aggressive and assertive behaviors? — 121
- Why behave assertively? — 122
- How assertive are you? — 123
- Why rights are Important — 125
- Optimizing your personal behavior — 126
- Learning to be assertive — 127

## Chapter 11
## Leadership and motivation — **129**

- Introduction — 130
- The problem with people — 130
- The hierarchy of human needs — 132
- Statistic analysis — 133
- What is leadership? — 135
- The Holy Grail of management — 135
- The tool box style — 140

## Chapter 12
## The Science of communication — **141**

- Introduction — 142
- Why do we communicate? — 142
- How communication works — 143
- The communication process — 145
- Coding the message — 146
- Choosing the right channel — 148
- Proxemics — 150
- Transactional analysis — 151
- Noise — 153
- Sensation vs perception vs knowing — 154
- Illusion and communication — 155
- So what's the problem? — 156

## Chapter 13
## Effective communication           159

- Introduction                       160
- Talking                            162
- Listening                          164
- Active listening                   166
- Feed back                          167
- Creativity and communications      170
- Gearing                            173

## Chapter 14
## Counseling and training           175

- Introduction                       176
- Counseling                         178
- Preparation                        180
- Choose the approach                181
- The six steps                      182
- On the job training                184
- Don't be a schoolteacher           186
- The three areas for on the job training   186
- Get prepared                       187
- The four-step Process              190

## Chapter 15
## Problem people                                           **191**

- Introduction                                              192
- Recognize that a problem exists                           192
- Reasons for problems                                      193
- Evidence of problems                                      193
- Basic management tools for solving problems               194
- Reacting to the problem employee                          194
- Key success factors                                       195
- What to do when all else fails                            196
- Practical examples of coaching                            197
- Practical examples of counseling                          198

## Chapter 16
## Positive discipline                                      **199**

- Introduction                                              200
- Discipline line                                           200
- Consistency                                               201
- Well communicated                                         201
- Reasonable and justifiable                                202
- Flexibility                                               202
- Immediacy                                                 203
- Privacy                                                   203
- The "Hot stove rule"                                      204
- Minor misdemeanors                                        205
- Serious disciplinary issues                               205
- Working within the system                                 207

## Chapter 17
## People planning    **209**

- Introduction — 210
- Get yourself informed — 212
- Typical development plan for people — 214
- Determine the correct management style to use — 215
- Style selection chart — 218
- People planning approach — 219
- Increase productivity through motivation — 221
- Building and maintaining relationships — 224
- Relationship channels — 224
- Tips on building good relationships — 225
- Your behavior — 227
- The super Z manager specification — 228

## Chapter 18
## Action for success    **229**

- Introduction — 230
- Management by objectives — 231
- The inevitability of change — 233
- Reducing resistance — 234
- Our first SMART objectives — 236
- Prepare a simple plan — 239
- Survival tips — 241

## *Foreword*

I have spent most of my working life in managerial positions in the demanding world of oil and gas plant construction and operations. I started as a lead engineer and moved onto project manager positions and even to director in a multinational company. So this book is very hands on management orientated. I have personally encountered most of the problems characterized in the book and had to deal with the solutions.

During my career there were limited assistance skill development initiatives and we just had to get on without. I was amazed to see how many top quality people were being promoted to management positions without even a briefing let alone a training course. Many failed for no fault of their own. For this reason, I developed the **Managers Toolbox** training series and this book.

I have been careful not to include too much management theory but it is important to understand something of how the art of management has developed. If this is not for you then skip over it; but you may be surprised about how interesting it is.

Everything in this book is achievable but may seem overwhelming as you read through. I strongly suggest that you read through the entire book without being too judgmental about the work needed to achieve all the potential objectives. The last chapter is called Action for Success and will help you use the book to develop a sensible personal development plan. You can then decide which chapters are more important than others. In some cases, you may classify chapters as reference points for the future and only return to them when specific problems arise.

Chris Thomas

# CHAPTER 1

# INTRODUCTION

| | |
|---|---:|
| • What is the problem? | 2 |
| • Why change at all? | 3 |
| • Why does change happen? | 4 |
| • Risks and benefits of change | 5 |
| • Typical changes | 6 |
| • Born to lead | 8 |
| • Benefits of becoming a better manager | 8 |
| • Benefits for your family | 9 |
| • Guaranteed to work | 10 |
| • About this book | 10 |

## What is the problem?

Most of my adult life has been spent working as a supervisor or manager on industrial projects throughout the world. As the years passed I have become more and more convinced that the supervisor is the most critical of all roles in industry. The success of companies in today's highly demanding and competitive world depends on the ability to achieve changes at all levels in the organization. The supervisor controls the key organizational ground that separates management from the workforce, which is fundamental to introducing and sustaining effective change.

Of course there are many excellent companies who realize this and have developed the supervisor role to its deserved status. However, it is remarkable that the others still do not recognize that the supervisor is a key manager in the organization.

Something is wrong!

Unfortunately, many supervisors are given their demanding roles without adequate preparation. People are commonly promoted into management and supervisory positions without being given the basic skills to be a manager. Although personal attributes and technical knowledge are important they are not enough by themselves for the new challenges. An effective manager will have improved job satisfaction and will enhance company performance.

Recent studies have shown that industrial supervisors are working at less than 60 % of their potential. This book is designed to release this potential in the following ways:

- To provide supervision with the basic management skills to support their work and to improve efficiency

- To demonstrate how this new knowledge and expertise can be practically applied in the work situation

Making the changes necessary to close the supervisor effectiveness gap will be a challenge and to make a smooth transition to success you will need the help that this book provides. In fact, I guarantee you success if you actively adopt my recommendations.

# Why change at all?

*I've been doing things this way for years. Nobody has complained. Why should I change?*

I have heard this many times and many people probably will have sympathy with this approach. It's a good question that needs a good response. Here are three good reasons.

OK we have to change!

### It's inevitable

Change will happen with or without your involvement. Change is a natural phenomenon of human beings and if you fight it, then you will lose.

### Survival

If you fight the concept of change you are in danger of being left behind or even left outside the system. This will create a serious threat to your personal career security.

## It's your responsibility

You have a personal and professional responsibility to others to create something better. Your fathers and grandfathers did it for you.

## For yourself

Change is challenging but also invigorating, as you will be involved and you will start achieving things. You will be surprised how that will cheer you up.

Still not convinced? Maybe your company is one of the few that have survived without change in today's world. If it has not happened then get prepared for it and when it comes it can often hit you like a tornado!

# Why does change happen?

Change has always been inevitable, but in these modern times it has reached epidemic levels. It is all around us like never before. What causes this to happen?

## Innovation

Man has always been innovative ever since pre-historic times. However, since the industrial revolution this process has been accelerated. Many governments, universities, companies, etc. have harnessed this innovate force into highly funded research and development programs. For example, the NASA space program has made major contributions in the fields of materials and electronics. These advances in technology have dramatically changed the roles of human beings in the industrial world. Machines now do work that used to be the domain of men. New skills have to be developed to meet these changes. Training and re-training will continue to be the way forward.

## Competition

We now talk about a global economy and the end of restrictive practices. Much of North America, Europe and the Far East have formed free trade areas. This process will continue and more and more countries will have to compete in this highly competitive world. This has forced a very aggressive approach to product prices, costs and profits. Look how pricing philosophy has developed over the years:

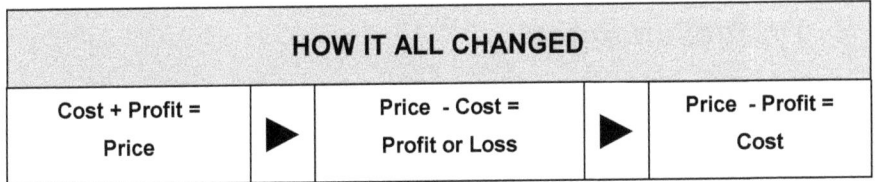

| HOW IT ALL CHANGED | | |
|---|---|---|
| Cost + Profit = Price | Price - Cost = Profit or Loss | Price - Profit = Cost |

The result of this is that cost has now become the key target to achieve.

## Customer pressure

Customers and clients are demanding more than ever before. Styles change and expectations are raised as we are increasingly being affected by television, advertising and modern marketing techniques. To survive we have to be flexible to change and be able to respond to market demands.

## *Risks and benefits of change*

There is no doubt that change has improved the living conditions of millions of people. Life expectancy is higher, reduced infant mortality and the quality of life are examples of the results of changes in medical and health care. We are more informed and involved in our future destinies due to advances in communication and education. Modern transportation has made the world a smaller place. All of these are normally accepted as changes for the good.

However, not all change is considered to be good by all people. Change has had its problems and has not been universally welcomed. New illnesses such as stress have entered our lives. Many people believe that the new approaches to life have eroded family values and a new age of decadence has been established.

Whatever your viewpoint, change is not going to stop. At least, if you embrace change and get involved in it then you can make it work for you.

## *Typical changes*

Let's look at the types of changes that you, as supervisors, are likely to be involved in as a result of the development of this dynamic global market that we are in.

| CHANGE | DESCRIPTION |
| --- | --- |
| DOWNSIZING | This is the process of reducing the company size. These programs usually involve efficiency improvements that optimize production. |
| OUTSOURCING | The object of outsourcing is to contract those activities considered as non-core to specialist companies so that the management can focus on the core activities. |
| WORKFORCE | Workforces need to be flexible and continually trained and re-trained. Multi-skilling and specialist groups are developed to improve efficiency. |

| CHANGE | DESCRIPTION |
|---|---|
| NEW PHILOSOPHIES | New philosophies are usually introduced as a result of take-overs or the arrival of a new management team. This involves adjusting to a new work culture and its associated changes. |
| QUALITY & ENVIRONMENTAL SYSTEMS | The implementation of ISO 9000 and 1400 series of standards and similar systems has created enormous changes in management procedures and practices. |
| COST REDUCTION AND EFFICIENCY PROGRAMS | These programs have been inevitable in our competitive world. Companies will search for all opportunities to maintain or improve company success. |
| SAFETY | Safety has dramatically moved from being a moral obligation to a fundamental company objective. This has involved new work practices and greater management participation. |
| VENDORS | Vendors are expected to meet new standards. Vendor databases are extended to include world-wide capability. |
| NEW MANAGEMENT SYSTEMS | General and specialized management systems are now commonly used. These could be Integrated Systems, JIT, ISO 9000, RCM, TQM, etc. |

All these changes are initiated by senior management and then filter down the hierarchy. In many cases the final implementation of these changes ends up the responsibility of the supervisor. So the today's supervisor needs to juggle many balls to succeed.

## Born to lead

Many people believe that good managers, like some good sportsmen, are born, not made. Fortunately research does not support this view. In fact, history shows us the damage caused by these so called natural leaders. We must be careful not to confuse charisma with leadership skills.

Of course some of us are endowed with more potential in some areas than others. For example, Adolf Hitler had enormous abilities to motivate but totally lacked any planning and organizational skills. So it is often a trade off.

Most top athletes have some natural endowment but it is the constant coaching and practice that brings success. The same is true for a good manager. Management skills can be learnt and practiced to perfection just like you do with your local tennis or golf pro. It will take time, effort, and determination but no one said it would be easy.

## Benefits of becoming a better manager

I mentioned earlier that change is good for you. What about the personal benefits to you in becoming a skilled manager. Let's look at these in more detail:

### You become more successful

In spite of what we say, we all love success for ourselves and our loved ones. It is just natural and it makes us feel good and I cannot think of a better benefit than this.

## You are in control

I prefer to be controlling my own destiny and not always following others. A good manager is always in control even in crisis situations. You get less unpleasant surprises and problems.

## You have more time available

Now you can have the luxury of time to think. How to make further improvements? You get more quality time with your family with less emergency call outs.

## You become more popular

Please forget about all this tough talk of a good manager has to be unpopular. That went out before sliced bread. I am not suggesting that you make popularity an objective but it will happen naturally by being a good manager. Believe me that working in a pleasant work environment takes some beating.

## You will be healthier

Industrial stress and its related diseases has become a major and world-wide problem. Good management training can be a major factor in reducing these problems.

# *Benefits for your family*

Wow, this is dangerous territory. Of course our family life is not structured as a company but there are many similarities. You need to plan and organize your family affairs and projects. On times you have to be a leader and be able to communicate at both adult and child levels. Most of us are positive about change when it comes to our families - we all want our children to do better than ourselves.

## Guaranteed to work

I guaranteed you that this book will work for you but only if you follow the advice given. I think it's the best product of its type on the market but it's not magic. I have designed the book in the hope that it becomes your life time friend and not just a one off read. How you use it, or don't use it, is up to you. You may find it interesting to read the whole book before making important judgements then you can go back and look at those chapters that can help you most.

Don't get overwhelmed and don't try to change the world in one day. The last chapter will help you put things into perspective and if followed correctly will guarantee you success.

## About this Book

Throughout this book notes I use the names supervisor and manager. If you like, you can add director too. They all mean the same thing. A supervisor is a manager.

The book chapters are in the following order:

- Part 1 consists of 4 chapters and describes the role and functions of a supervisor

- Part 2 consists of 3 chapters and covers managing yourself

- Part 3 consists of 6 chapters and deals with the skills for managing others

- Part 4 consists of 2 chapters and covers the management tools at your disposal and how to create a personal action plan.

The next page has a detailed flow diagram showing all the chapters and how they fit together.

Basic Management Skills — Introduction

## PART 1
## ROLE AND FUNCTIONS

*Surveys have shown that poor role definition is a major cause of industrial stress. In addition, people without direction and objective functions will never perform to their full potential. This group of chapters addresses these problems and builds the base for the development of management skills*

1. INTRODUCTION
2. ROLES & RESPONSIBILITIES
3. MANAGEMENT BY OBJECTIVES
4. THE ART OF PLANNING
5. HOW TO GET ORGANIZED
6. CONTROL FUCTION

## PART 2
## MANAGING YOURSELF

*A pre-requisite for managing others is being able to manage yourself. Poor time management alone can waste 20% of our time*

7. TIME MANAGEMENT
8. MAKING DECISIONS
9. GIVING INSTRUCTIONS
10. ASSERTIVE BEHAVIOR

## PART 3
## MANAGING OTHERS

*These chapters demonstrate how we can all apply these basic principles with immediate results*

11. LEADERSHIP & MOTIVATION
12. THE SCIENCE OF COMMUNICATION
13. EFFECTIVE COMMUNICATION
14. COUNSELING AND TRAINING
15. PROBLEM PEOPLE
16. POSITIVE DISCIPLINE

## PART 4
## PERSONAL DEVELOPMENT PLAN

17. PEOPLE PLANNING
18. ACTION FOR SUCCESS

*These chapters are all about converting problems into opportunities for improved efficiency and productivity. How to implement changes in a sensible and effective manner*

# CHAPTER 2

# THE ROLE AND RESPONSIBILITY OF A SUPERVISOR

| | |
|---|---|
| • Who is a supervisor? | 14 |
| • What is a supervisor? | 15 |
| • What are the resources other than himself? | 16 |
| • Which is the most important resource? | 17 |
| • The four directions | 17 |
| • The management cycle | 18 |
| • Management levels | 21 |
| • Supervising means supervising | 22 |
| • Task analysis | 23 |
| • Barriers to the effectiveness of the supervisor | 25 |
| • Destroying the barriers | 27 |

## Who is a supervisor?

A good starting point for any course on supervision or management is that of identity. All effective managers will be able to respond to the question **WHO AM I?** In a clear manner that is acceptable to himself, his superiors, his peers and the people who work for him.

Many supervisors are promoted from within the organization, with many coming from the workforce, and this in itself causes both cultural and practical problems. Managers often find themselves in direct control of their friends, ex co-workers and others who share the same habits, customs and social activities. In many cases new supervisors will have little in common with their new management colleagues.

We are all managers but really, who are we?

In spite of all this the supervisor must continually look in both directions and act as the link between top down and bottom up interests. This can be even more problematic at the supervisor-worker interface, which has been a traditional conflict area. In fact, managers have to look in four directions, as we will discuss later.

For success a manager must satisfy the needs of his bosses and his subordinates and maintain his:

- Personal integrity

- Credibility

There is solid evidence from recent studies that the non-understanding of individual roles and responsibilities is a significant cause of industrial stress. A key objective in this chapter is to develop a list of tasks and responsibilities that meet management needs but also make sense to you as individual managers.

## *What is a supervisor?*

What is meant by the terms manager and supervisor? Simply stated they are the people that:

- Get things done with resources other than just themselves

- Being responsible for more than they can do alone.

Of course, managers will always have non-supervisory tasks to do such as reports to write, meetings, etc.

All organizations will have important non-supervisory personnel. However, the key difference between them and supervisors and managers is that they do not *get things done through others.*

One of the main problems for first time supervisors is that they find it hard to accept that **they can no longer do it themselves**. Most workers who are promoted into first line supervisor jobs are selected because of their high technical and hands-on skills. In many cases, the promoted worker was the best worker in the crew. However, to succeed as a manager you must avoid doing the work yourself except in emergency or training circumstances.

The other key difference is that workers and other non-managers usually approach jobs one at a time with the simple objective of getting them finished. However, a supervisor has to take control of numerous tasks that need to be performed at the same time. This is not an easy change to make.

The promotion of a supervisor from the ranks is a risky process because if the new manager cannot handle these fundamental changes then the company has not only gained an ineffective supervisor but also lost one of their best workers.

Some managers never learn how to delegate correctly or to plan their work and end up trying to do everything themselves and in many cases with their subordinates looking on in amazement. These managers will always be under-performers and usually get weeded out in efficiency programs.

Once a new supervisor has learned to think as a supervisor instead of as a worker, life as a manager starts to make sense.

## *Supervisor = Manager*

So what is the difference between a supervisor and a manager?

Answer: In terms of management functions - NOTHING - except their positions in the organization. As we will see later the extent that particular techniques are employed will vary at different management levels but the basics are the same for chief executives as they are for supervisors

## What are the resources other than himself?

These resources can be summarized as:

- People
- Money
- Materials
- Equipment

## Which is the most important resource?

- People can express all other resources in terms of money

- Machines cannot survive without people

- People outnumber machines

- Machines do as they are told - people don't

- People cost around 5 times more than any other resource

So it is quite clear that a manager most important priority should be to manage people effectively.

## The four directions

There is no doubt that the common assumption that the most important people to a supervisor are his subordinates is true. However, his effectiveness will be improved significantly if he visualizes his role in the concept of four directions. These are upward, downward, sideways and inward.

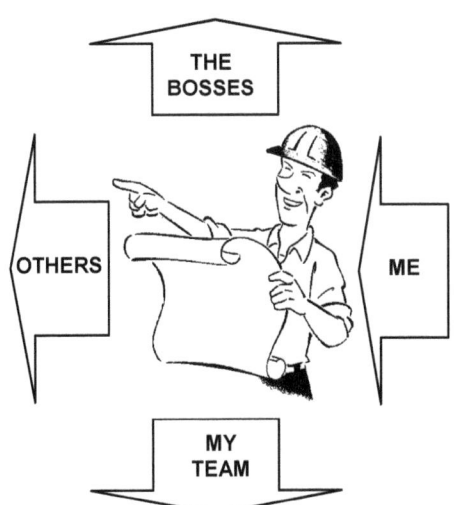

## Upward

In addition to managing others a supervisor is also a follower. He must consider the needs and requirements of his boss, which should always be consistent with the company's objectives.

## Downward

The management of subordinates is the most difficult and demanding direction for a supervisor and is the main theme of this book.

## Sideways

A supervisor must work in harmony with his peers. In other words, the people in other departments or organizations, who are not in his own direct management line.

## Inward

It is essential that supervisor be able to manage himself effectively. His personal performance will create respect from others and set an example for others to follow.

# *The management cycle*

There are four basic functions of all managers regardless of how technical or complex the work involved may be. The managerial content of a supervisory position is the same whether the person is a cleaning services supervisor, the chief engineer of a technical division, a production line foreman, or even a senior churchman, such as a bishop who supervises numerous priests and lay workers.

These same basic functions apply to all levels in the organization from the first line supervisor through middle-level management onto the top management levels. Nor does it matter in what kind of organization one is working because these four basic functions are the same whether the manager is involved in an industrial or commercial enterprise, a nonprofit organization, government offices, schools, or a hospital. ALL managers performs the same basic functions, which are as follows:

| FUNCTION | ACTIVITY |
|---|---|
| 1<br><br>TO PLAN | THINKING, THINKING, THINKING<br><br>• WHAT are we going to do?<br>• WHEN are we going to do it?<br>• WHY are we going to do it? |
| 2<br><br>TO ORGANIZE | GETTING IT SORTED<br><br>• HOW are we going to do it?<br>• WHERE are we going to do it?<br>• WHO is going to do it? |
| 3<br><br>TO IMPLEMENT | PEOPLE IN ACTION<br><br>• WHAT motivation will they need?<br>• WHAT training will they need?<br>• WHAT support will they need? |
| 4<br><br>TO CONTROL | EVALUATE AND MODIFY<br><br>• HOW will we know how we are doing?<br>• WHERE are we going?<br>• WHERE are the opportunities and threats? |

These four functions form what is commonly known as the **supervisory or management cycle**.

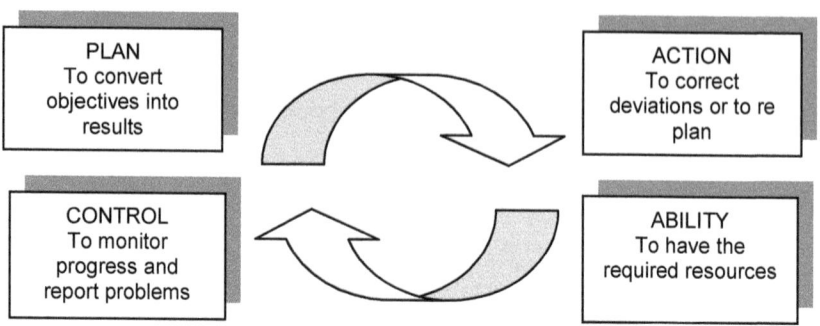

However, in order for the cycle to work effectively other elements are required, these are:

- Company policy
- Leadership
- Communication
- Personal effectiveness

This process works in an ever-changing world. Even if you repeat exactly the same task every day you will find that things will vary. For example, company goals may change or your people may change for better or for worse. A good supervisor will always be adapting himself to these changes.

At this point you only need to understand the concept of the management cycle. We will go into the details of each of the functions involved in later chapters.

# Management levels

Although the management functions never change there are different levels in their application. These are usually classified using three management levels.

## First-line supervision

Hi! I am the Divisional Manager

This level covers the direct supervision of craft-level personnel. Managers in this group are often called supervisors, team leaders, foremen, etc.

## Middle-level management

This level supervises the first-line managers. These managers include the department managers, superintendents and controllers of specialist groups.

## Top-level management

This group supervises the activities of middle management and other specialist groups. Work titles such as CEO, executive and administrator are common at the top management level.

Notice how the words manager, management, supervision and supervisor are used freely at each level.

All three supervisory levels carry out the four management functions of Planning, Organizing, Leading and Controlling but with different emphasis.

The **first-line supervisor** has to get the job done. This involves a considerable amount of time checking work quality, supervising job procedures, on the job training, maximizing productivity, etc.

**Middle-management** is not directly involved in getting the job done. This level is largely a support operation that ensures that top down management policies are passed on and achieved but also to provide bottom up support to the front line supervisors.

The **top-level supervisor** usually called a manager is basically a planner. He sets the mission statements, corporate policies and develops work strategies concerned with performance, long-term planning, and how to achieve the company's goals.

At each level the number of people being directly supervised decreases. For example, a supervisor may have 20 subordinates to control but the CEO (Chief Executive Officer) may only have 3 or 4. However, the CEO will have indirect responsibility for all the employees. So you can see that as you get higher in the organization then planning time increases but the level of people contact decreases.

## MBWA (Management by walkabout)

One of the most powerful tools that any manager has is MBWA, which is the activity of ***directly*** "supervising" his subordinates. Front line managers should spend around 45% of their time involved with MBWA but they rarely do.

Hewlett Packard (HP) are attributed with formalizing MBWA in the 1970s and using it as a highly successful method of involving employees, MBWA was later advocated by Tom Peters, the esteemed management guru, in his famed book "In Search of Excellence,"

MBWA does not mean just wandering around aimlessly and engaging in pointless chatter. The following are good examples of MBWA time:

- Walking the job
- On the job training
- Discussing work with subordinates
- Counseling subordinates
- Asking for ideas, suggestions and even criticism

The time spent with your subordinates is the key to your success as a supervisor. If you have not enough time to be with your people then you should ask your boss to change your title because you are not a supervisor. If you spend too little time in this key activity then you are not working at your full potential irrespective of how experienced or qualified you may be. This applies to all levels of management including CEO's.

There are so many benefits to being on the job with your people. These are a few but maybe you can think of more.

- You are visible. Your people will realize that you are interested

- You can help solve problems as they occur. You now become useful to your people.

- You can build relationships, which is a key factor in team building

- You will instinctively know where the problems are

The following chapters in this book are designed to assist you in optimizing your time with your people and to maximize your effectiveness with them. Of all the things that you will learn in this book MBWA is NUMBER 1 in terms of importance and effectiveness.

## *Task analysis*

In this part we are going to look at a very general analysis of the way a supervisor uses his time in comparison with an industry survey done in the USA. This will be an interesting view on what may be necessary to be done to optimize your role as a supervisor. Please note that the figures stated in the following chart are a guide and not a standard to achieve. Each industry and country will make different demands on the supervisor. You can compare your own performance by completing the boxes in the following chart.

| ACTIVITY | NORMAL | OPTIMAL |
|---|---|---|
| **PLANNING**<br><br>- Setting group objectives and priorities<br>- Identifying your groups' workload<br>- Scheduling the workload<br>- Determining levels of labor, equipment, tools and materials<br>- Preparing work scopes for individual tasks<br>- Determining group facilities | 10 %<br>5 hours<br>per week | 20 %<br>10 hours<br>per week |
|  | Insert your hours here: ||

| ORGANISATION<br><br>• Specifying job skills<br>• Allocating resources<br>• Authorizing overtime<br>• Ordering materials<br>• Ordering outside services<br>• Requesting plant and equipment<br>• Coordinating assistance from other groups | 27%<br>13.5 hours<br>per week | 15%<br>7.5 hours<br>per week |
|---|---|---|
| | Insert your hours here: ||
| SUPERVISION<br><br>• Giving job instructions<br>• Resolving restrictions to progress<br>• Maintaining and improving productivity<br>• Assessing individual and group performance<br>• Maintaining discipline line<br>• Induction and training of crew<br>• Counseling group | 24%<br>12 hours<br>per week | 45%<br>22.5 hours<br>per week |
| | Insert your hours here: ||
| CONTROL<br><br>• Setting quality and production standards<br>• Establish reporting procedures<br>• Evaluating performance<br>• Provide planning feedback | 2%<br>1 hour<br>per week | 10%<br>5 hours<br>per week |
| | Insert your hours here: ||
| ADMINISTRATION<br><br>• Filling in forms or writing reports for others<br>• Providing information for accountants, administrators<br>• Trying to make computers work<br>• General office work | 37%<br>18.5 hours<br>per week | 10%<br>5 hours<br>per week |
| | Insert your hours here: ||
| TOTALS: | 100% | 100% |

It is clear that Mr. Average Supervisor has some work to do. Throughout this book we will be using the information generated in this chapter to help us reduce the barriers facing supervisors and to improve efficiency.

If you add up all the hours on the last chart you will get 50 hours. This is around 10 hours more than normal working hours – in other words it is OVERTIME. A major objective for us must be to eliminate regular overtime.

Of course, a supervisor's job is never going to be 8 to 4 or 9 to 5 and irregular hours and call outs will always occur but regular overtime only achieves short-term gains.

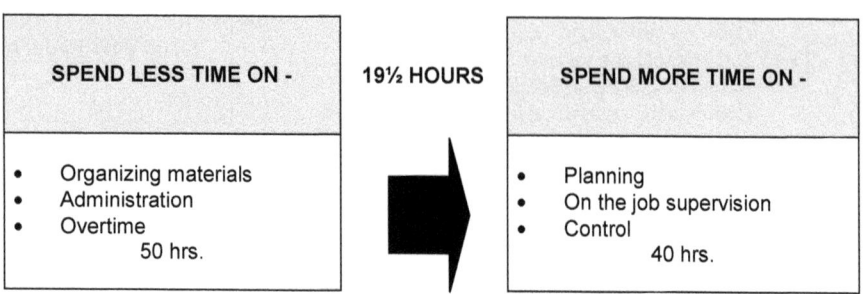

| SPEND LESS TIME ON - | 19½ HOURS | SPEND MORE TIME ON - |
|---|---|---|
| • Organizing materials<br>• Administration<br>• Overtime<br>50 hrs. | ➡ | • Planning<br>• On the job supervision<br>• Control<br>40 hrs. |

The above exercise is based on information relevant to first line supervisors but the principles apply to other levels of management. Of course, a middle manager with 3 subordinates will not normally need to spend the same direct supervising time as a supervisor with 20 workers under his control. However, there are many well known managers that are convinced that their success is due to being closely involved with their people.

## *Barriers to the effectiveness of the supervisor*

### Poorly defined or no job description

You can only perform your duties if someone has clearly told you what they are! It is incredible how many companies assume that a supervisor role is so obvious that it does not need further explanation. Others believe that rigid job descriptions restrict creativity so now we have to add *artist* to the list of capabilities of the poor supervisor.

It is a fundamental right of both the manager and the person being managed to clearly understand what is expected from each other.

## Over involvement in operational work

Operational work is work that could be done by your subordinates. In many cases, a supervisor needs to do operational work as a training demonstration for a relatively inexperienced group. However, most supervisors prefer doing to thinking and it is easy to become over involved in operational work.

## Doing the work of other departments

Supervisors are action men that need to react to the daily pressures from the work face. If other departments do not provide the support required then supervisors tend *to do it themselves*. It is very common to see supervisors acting as materials expeditors, production assistants, etc. in addition to their normal duties. In time, these duties become part of the supervisors' informal job description.

## Lack of management skills

Most supervisors are appointed one day and are expected to perform all the complex tasks of management the next day without any form of training or preparation. This is not fair to the individual or an effective strategy for management.

# *Destroying the barriers*

## Sort out your role and responsibilities

This chapter should have sufficient information and guidance to allow you to evaluate your present role. To be effective the supervisor whether he likes it or not, has to meet management expectations, which are based on corporate goals. In consequence, it is important to talk to your boss about your role. In particular it would be well worth while completing the above chart jointly with your boss. It could take an hour or so but this could prove to be the best spent time in your working life.

The rest of this book will give you the essential tools to be able to make the necessary changes.

## Improve your personal resources

It is very clear that the role of an effective supervisor is very demanding and that you need considerable personal skills and resources to be successful. These can be grouped as shown on the following chart:

| Group | Skills |
|---|---|
| Knowledge | - Knowledge of the role and responsibilities<br>- Knowledge of company policies and objectives<br>- Technical knowledge of the work to be done |
| Managing yourself | - Effective personal behavior<br>- Ability to think positively<br>- Good time management<br>- To make decisions |
| Managing others | - To motivate others<br>- Training others |
| Communication | - To give information<br>- To give instructions<br>- To listen effectively<br>- To improve communications<br>- To make presentations |

# CHAPTER 3

# MANAGEMENT BY OBJECTIVES

| | |
|---|---|
| • Introduction | 30 |
| • What are SMART objectives? | 31 |
| • How it works | 34 |
| • The performance commitment | 36 |
| • The 80 / 20 principle (Pareto) | 37 |
| • The main benefits of MBO | 39 |
| • Murphy's law | 40 |

Basic Management Skills                                    Management by Objectives

## Introduction

Management by Objectives (MBO) is a simple and powerful method of managing operations at every level within an organization based on defined goals that are consistent with the overall policy and objectives. However, MBO is often open to abuse when it becomes over-complicated and highly bureaucratic. This can result in a damaging process of internal politics and possible open conflict. MBO can produce amazing results but to do so MBO needs high levels of respect, trust and teamwork with effective and honest communication.

I am a SMART manager!

MBO can be effective in a major corporation such as Microsoft, in a small business or even in your personal life. The essence of MBO is all about being focused on GOALS that are consistent with your company's business objectives. Goals are very important for individuals and society because without them there is a tendency to lose direction and end in failure. You only have to watch the news bulletins to see the number of big companies and institutions that slip into bad times and even bankruptcy. A more dramatic example are the young people that drift from school into drugs and crime or the increasing number of retired or redundant workers, who have lost their spirit to live. Life is all about GOALS - and the spirit of MBO is all about achieving your objectives.

The most effective way to use MBO is as a part of a company policy and a well-defined system. If your company has such a system then you should embrace it and make every effort to make it work. It will be well worth the effort. If you don't have a formal MBO program in your company then you can start your own because the basic principles can be applied almost anywhere.

## *What are SMART objectives?*

In the first place, we need to understand how to determine and evaluate our goals or objectives. To assist us in this, I have invented a list of possible goals or objectives, which we are going to evaluate.

1. To increase output as much as possible

2. To reduce accidents

3. To increase output by 60%

4. To improve performance by sacking anyone who shows a bad attitude

5. To reduce accidents by 10% over the next 6 months

6. To increase output by 1% over the next year

7. To reduce costs by 50% over the next 6 months

There are numerous methods to evaluate objectives. We need to identify the real objectives and discard those that are merely statements. A perfect objective is rare but it should perform well against the requirements of the **SMART** test.

| SMART OBJECTIVES ARE: ||
|---|---|
| **S**<br><br>SPECIFIC | If an objective is precise then there is only one way in which it can be interpreted. |
| **M**<br><br>MEASURABLE | This means: can our progress in achieving the objective be measured as we proceed? This is difficult to achieve as it is often necessary to wait until the end to measure. |
| **A**<br><br>ACCEPTABLE | This means acceptable to the organization or the people that have to do it or society in general. Of course, this would include illegal acts or morally or ethically unacceptable actions. |
| **R**<br><br>REALISTIC | In other words can it be done? Of course, you need to know the subject and the problems well to make this judgement and this is why so many senior management objectives fail.<br><br>It used to be thought that you should set objectives at slightly higher levels than you actually require. The idea was that people would extend themselves further. This is now considered wrong because people do not try so hard if they think an objective is not realistic. |
| **T**<br><br>TIME RELATED | When are you going to achieve it and when will you start? They say that road to heaven is paved with good intentions. Without time the objective lacks commitment. |

Let's look at our list of possible objectives and see what results we can get with the SMART test.

| RESULTS | |
|---|---|
| **SPECIFIC** | Numbers 1, 2 and 4 fail (how do you define a bad attitude?). |
| **MEASURABLE** | 5, 6 and 7 are measurable by comparing performance against rate of progress required.<br><br>2 and 3 could be measured at the end of specified periods.<br><br>1 and 4 fail for practical reasons. |
| **ACCEPTABLE** | 6 may be agreed to by the work force but not management.<br><br>3 would not be acceptable to the unions or an industrial tribunal<br><br>7 would probably keep the accountants happy but not those who have to do it. |
| **REALISTIC** | 3 and 7 are almost certainly not realistic<br><br>5 and 6 may be - more information is required |
| **TIME** | 5, 6 and 7 have times allocated. The rest no. |

| OBJECTIVES SUMMARY | 1 | 2 | 3 | 4 | 5 | 6 | 7 |
|---|---|---|---|---|---|---|---|
| SPECIFIC | ✗ | ✗ | ✓ | ✗ | ✓ | ✓ | ✓ |
| MEASURABLE | ✗ | ✓ | ✓ | ✗ | ✓ | ✓ | ✓ |
| ACCEPTABLE | ✓ | ✓ | ✗ | ✓ | ✓ | ✗ | ✗ |
| REALISTIC | ✓ | ✓ | ✗ | ✓ | ✓ | ✓ | ✗ |
| TIME | ✗ | ✗ | ✗ | ✓ | ✓ | ✓ | ✓ |

## How it works

MBO is a huge hierarchy of goals at many levels, which start at the top and become more specific at lower levels. It is like a giant cascade where the goals at lower levels achieve the requirements of the goals at higher levels. All the phases of the MANAGEMENT CYCLE work together link these levels and specifics into a whole (a "Systems Approach"). However, the entire system depends on clearly stated goals and priorities from the top. If there is misunderstanding due to vagueness or ambivalence then all the other levels will become corrupted causing almost certain failure.

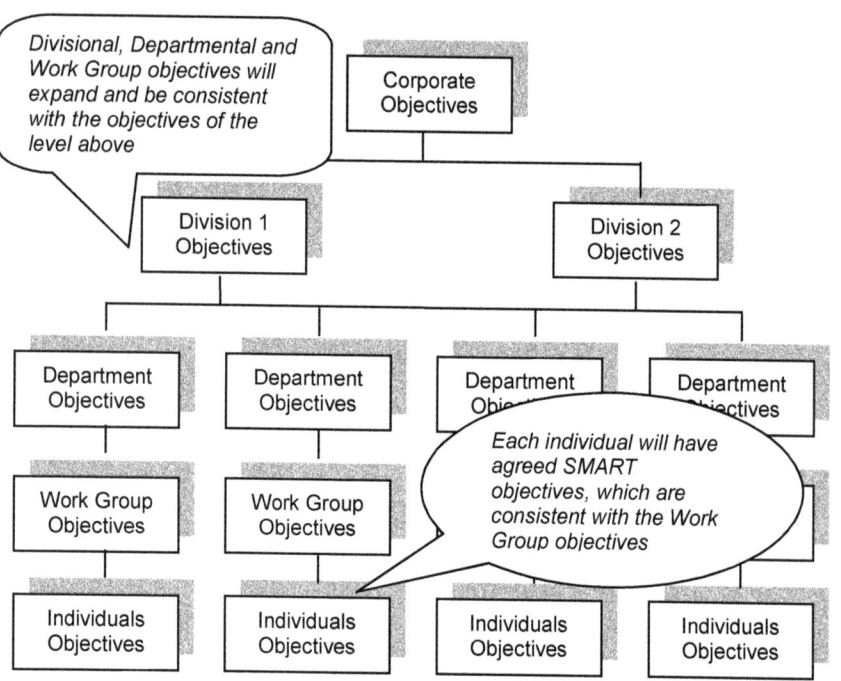

Another good way to look at MBO is as a large inter-related network of cells, where each cell represents a personal commitment between two people. However, it is important to note that this process is not an intellectual exercise, it's all about **ACTION**. Let's see how the stages work:

| STAGE | KEY ACTIVITIES | COMMENTS |
|---|---|---|
| STAGE 1 | TOP MANAGER SETS ULTIMATE OBJECTIVES | These objectives tend to be general but they must be precise and clear |
| STAGE 2 | SENIOR MANAGERS DELEGATE OBJECTIVES TO NEXT LEVEL DEPARTMENTS | As the objective pass down the levels they become more specific and will become really SMART (see notes on SMART objectives below). Senior managers co-ordinate their objectives to ensure that there is cross-fertilization of ideas and approaches |
| STAGE 3 | LINE MANAGER ANALYSES AND PREPARES OBJECTIVES FOR HIS DEPARTMENT<br><br>LINE MANAGER DECIDES ON HOW AND TO WHOM TO DELEGATE WORK WITHIN HIS DEPARTMENT<br><br>LINE MANAGER SETS OBJECTIVES FOR EACH INDIVIDUAL GROUP LEADER AND SUPERVISOR<br><br>LINE MANAGER FINALISES ALL OBJECTIVES AND SETS UP FEED-BACK CONTROL METHOD | **CELL INPUT**<br>The specific objectives set by the manager for the subordinate<br><br>**CELL ACTIVITIES**<br>1. Manager defines the subordinates objectives<br>2. Objectives are discussed<br>3. Modifications are considered<br>4. Objectives are agreed<br>5. Implementation is reviewed<br>6. Feed-back procedure agreed<br><br>**CELL OUTPUT**<br>Action plan with a written commitment |
| STAGE 4 | GROUP LEADER OR SUPERVISOR IMPLEMENTS THE PLAN | Managers must DELEGATE work to the workforce and not to simply ASSIGN the tasks. Delegation means clear communication, on the job training, counseling, motivating and being on the job with your group |
| STAGE 5 | MONITOR, ADJUST PLANS AS REQUIRED | Plans have to be constantly reviewed and adjusted to suit reality. Positive feedback allows us to take corrective action and update the MBO system. ( Don't forget MURPHY - see notes on MURPHY'S LAW at the end of this section – they are quite amusing) |

## *Performance commitment*

This is the power house of the MBO process where the specific goals are agreed jointly by the employee and his supervisor such that both clearly understand their obligations and what is to be achieved over an agreed time period (a month, quarter, year). This is often referred to as a **performance commitment** or agreement and is the basic building block of the MBO system. It is important to note that this is a commitment and should not be confused with a Job Description.

The MBO system links all these individual commitments into a consistent and coordinated hierarchy that manages the organization.

The following notes will help you get the best out of these agreements:

1. Do not use scraps of paper for your MOB exercises; use the sample forms at the end of this chapter as a guide. Good documentation shows that you are serious and it is much easier to control. In addition, note that it has been proven that people take typewritten information more seriously than hand-written notes.

2. Do not force your prepared objectives onto your subordinates. Discuss the objectives and their implications and actively involve them by asking for opinions and suggestions. Be prepared to compromise without jeopardizing higher level objectives. Your task is to get a willing and enthusiastic participant who will take part **ownership** of the objectives.

3. Make sure that your subordinate understands what is required of him. In a later section we will discuss COMMUNICATIONS and you will see how easy it is to fail in this area. You will also learn that good communication takes time so make sure you plan your cell meetings.

## *The 80 / 20 principle*

How many times have you heard people complain that. . . ?

**" A small group of people have all the power . . . "**

Or

**" Only a small part of the population seems to have all the money while the rest of us struggle to survive "**

You hear these things all over the world. An Italian economist at the beginning of the century called Alfredo **PARETO** discovered that a large proportion of the results come from a small proportion of causes. This is often called the 80 / 20 law because so many of the results have been in this magnitude. The PARETO principle or law can be applied to all human situations. Some good examples of the PARETO law are:

- 20 % of the people of Monrovia own 80% of the land

- 18% of the drivers cause 85% of the accidents

- 78% of the breakdowns are caused by 22% of the machines

- 90% of the management problems are caused by 25% of a supervisor's activities

This means that all things are not equal. For example, if you want to reduce accidents then you must spend more time and effort on the 18% of the drivers that cause the problem and less on the other 82%. Although this may seem obvious it is surprising that the differences in importance can be so high.

In summary the PARETO law tells us that if we devote the same time and energy to each of our activities then the following will result:

- 80% of your time will only produce 20% of your results

- 20% of your time will produce 80% of your results

The 20% that produce the 80% result is called the **VITAL FEW** and are obviously your **KEY ACTIVITIES**. The 80% that produces the 20% result is known as the **TRIVIAL MANY** and these are clearly not your key activities.

| VITAL FEW | TRIVIAL MANY |
|---|---|

The PARETO principle is very useful in helping us with our management problems. Obviously we need to use the idea with care as your activities will need examination and will not always fit the 80/20 pattern. However, it is an important concept in identifying the key areas that need additional attention. It is clear from the following examples of possible PARETO situations that it is very important to select our objectives carefully so that we can concentrate on the big problems first.

| SITUATION | A PARETO SITUATION COULD BE: |
|---|---|
| STORES | 20% (maybe) of all items in the store account for 80% (maybe) of the cost of the total inventory |
| PERSONNEL | A few people that work for you cause nearly all your personnel problems |
| DOWNTIME | A small number of machines (maybe a particular make or those working in the same working conditions) cause twice as many problems as the others |
| QUALITY | A small number of items account for the majority of the faults |

# The main benefits of MBO

## Keeps us all focused

It maintains focus on what we are trying to achieve. The objective will always bring us back on track, as it is very easy to lose your way in the management process.

## Keeps us all consistent

MOB ensures that even the lowest level objectives are positively linked and consistent with the company's main business objectives.

## Involves everyone

MBO is an excellent example of *Top Down Bottom Up* management in action. Although the initial objectives are the result of Top Down management, the final result will be agreed objectives, which adds the Bottom Up element

MBO is good for everybody

## Its good people management

MBO embodies all the ingredients for good people management. This will become clearer in later chapters.

# MURPHY'S LAW

The following selection of so-called business laws may appear amusing but each has a serious implication to it. Good management practices are your only protection from these laws.

| | |
|---|---|
| MURPHY'S LAW | If anything can go wrong, it will, and. . <br> 1. It will go wrong at the worst possible time <br> 2. Anything you plan will cost more and take longer <br> 3. To fix anything requires a tool that you don't have |
| MURFO'S JELLY BREAD PHENOMENON | Jelly-bread falls on a carpet jelly side down 100% of the time (despite laws of probability) |
| NON-RECIPROCAL LAWS OF EXPECTATIONS | 1. Negative expectations yield negative results <br> 2. Positive expectations yield negative results |
| LEWIS'S LAW | No matter how long you shop for an item, after you buy it, it will be on sale somewhere cheaper |
| THE FIRST LAW OF AERODYNAMICS | When the airplane you are on is late then your connecting flight is always on time |
| JOHNSON'S COSMIC OBSERVATION | The other line always moves faster. |
| OSBORN'S LAW OF CALCULATIONS | 1. Variables won't <br> 2. Constants aren't |
| THE TRANSPORTATION AXIOM | Truck deliveries that normally take one day, take five when you're waiting |

| | |
|---|---|
| COMPUTER AND PROGRAMMING AXIOMS | 1. Any program, when run, is obsolete.<br>2. The uselessness of any program is directly proportional to the need for it<br>3. All programs expand to fill all available memory<br>4. Program complexity grows until it exceeds the capability of the programmer to use or maintain it<br>5. The critical error in a program is always discovered exactly six months after the installation of the program |
| THE MACHINEMANSHIP OSTULATE | When any machine fails, it does so at the most inconvenient time. |
| LAW OF SELECTIVE GRAVITY | An object will fall so as to do the most damage |
| GEORGE'S DEDUCTION | When all else fails, read the instructions |
| SELMAN'S SECOND OBSERVATION | If enough data is collected, anything can be proved with statistics |
| PARKINSON'S LAWS | 1. Work expands to fill the time available for its completion.<br>2. Expenditures rise to meet income.<br>3. Scientific progress varies inversely with the number of journals and articles published.<br>4. The number of people in a work group tends to increase regardless of the work to be done.<br><br>Officials in any bureaucracy create work for each other (and need for larger staff) at a rate equal to the square of their total number (which, by formula, keeps increasing). |

| | |
|---|---|
| THE PETER PRINCIPLE: | In any hierarchy every employee tends to rise to his level of incompetence. This means that:<br>1. In time, incompetents occupy all positions.<br>2. Good work is done by lower-level people who have not yet reached their level of incompetence |
| SPECIALISATION | A specialist learns more and more about less and less until he knows everything about nothing |
| CHEOP'S AXIOM | Nothing ever gets built on schedule or within budget |
| LAWS OF COMMITTEEOLOGY | 1. Length of the meeting rises with the square of the number present<br>2. Time spent on an agenda item varies in inverse proportion to its importance or clarity |
| BOREN'S LAWS OF BUREAUCRACY | 1. If in doubt MUMBLE<br>2. If in trouble DELEGATE |
| THE ARMY AXIOM | Any order that can be misunderstood will be misunderstood |

**AND THE BEST OF THE LOT**

| | |
|---|---|
| 'TOOLE'S OBSERVATION | Murphy was an optimist! |

# CHAPTER 4

# THE ART OF PLANNING

| | | |
|---|---|---|
| • | The concept of planning | 44 |
| • | The basic planning process | 46 |
| • | Objectives | 46 |
| • | Get the facts | 47 |
| • | Evaluate alternatives | 48 |
| • | Develop the work scope | 51 |
| • | Prepare the plan | 52 |
| • | Activity lists | 52 |
| • | Bar charts | 54 |
| • | Dependencies | 58 |
| • | Action lists | 60 |
| • | Networks | 62 |

## The concept of planning

Every time we make a decision of any kind we become planners but as the process is so rapid we are not conscious of it. Every list of things to do (For  example: a shopping list for the supermarket) is a basic planning exercise.

Your annual holiday can often be a significant planning exercise if you choose to leave your home to go away. Just think of the planning activities involved in this. Don't forget that it does not have to be put on paper to be a plan - the mental process is the important issue.

Unfortunately planning has a bad name with supervisors and with the groups of people that actually do the work. Planning is seen as a remote activity done by people that know little about the real world. This is so often true, but this is a problem with people not with planning. The truth is that:

---

**PLANNERS WILL ALMOST ALWAYS OUT PERFORM NON PLANNERS**

PLANNING IS NOT A GUARANTEE OF SUCCESS BUT IT DOES PROVIDE THE BEST CHANCE THAT YOU HAVE FOR SUCCESS

---

So what are the problems associated with planning that cause these barriers:

| COMMON PROBLEMS WITH PLANNING ||
|---|---|
| It is not understood | This is true and one of our objectives is to correct this |
| It is mentally demanding | This is correct and no apologies will be given. You are all clever people or you would not be where you are today. This makes your job more interesting |
| It needs commitment | This absolutely correct and we will discuss why |
| It has a poor record | This is not strictly true but it does appear this way. So many projects overrun or end up with other grave problems. It is true that the average supervisor or worker has little confidence in planners. The problem is always the planners and not planning, as there are the millions of examples of successful planning. E.g. the NASA programs |
| Too management related | People think that only engineers and senior managers are related to planning. Not true! |

> Don't forget that **PLANNING** is about **ACTION** not information.
> **SUPERVISION** is also about **ACTION**.
>
> So **PLANNING** should be your best **FRIEND**.

Planning is natural and it is simple. This view may conflict with what you have been told or seen. It is important to remember that our world is full of people that love to complicate, invent buzzwords and create specialist worlds. I hope that this chapter will show how easy planning really is.

## The basic planning process

All plans from simple one-page documents through to complex projects such as landing a man on the moon share the same basic steps, which are:

- Set SMART Objectives

- Get the facts

- Evaluate alternatives

- Develop the work scope

- Prepare the plan

- Sell the plan

Of course the majority of planning done by supervisors will be a mental process or at most the preparation of a work list. However, these will involve the basic steps even if you do them almost subconsciously. However, every now and again we all need to plan a bigger more complex project, which it is important to get right. Usually, these need a little more than a list and the bar chart will be needed. In any case the rest of this chapter shows you how to approach these projects and enhancing your chances of success.

## Objectives

The planning process has been described as:

> **DEFINING THE STEPS TO TURN AN OBJECTIVE INTO A RESULT**

It is amazing how many people start off projects or tasks without real objectives or knowing what they want to achieve. Valid objectives are the first requirements in both the management and the planning process. MBO (Management by Objectives) is the powerful method that we discussed in an earlier chapter that includes the SMART method of establishing effective objectives. If you have any doubts about the importance or how to develop your own SMART objectives then please go to the MBO chapter again.

Of course we must prioritize our objectives by using the PARETO method or by other logic thought processes. Setting priorities is a vital part of a supervisor's responsibilities. You cannot do everything at once so you have to decide on which actions are more time important than others are. It is important to think before acting or you will fall into the trap of giving priority to the last thing that comes into your mind. The following are useful tools that can help you develop priorities.

## *Get the facts*

Once you have determined the SMART objectives then you can start to evaluate the work that needs to be done. This sounds obvious but many work lists are incomplete or inaccurate with the result that work is not planned and disrupts the progress of the project. Find out what the facts are, never assume things. Don't forget that it is not only technical things that matter, as there are many other factors such as weather, availability of materials and labor, etc.

## Evaluate alternatives

There are usually alternative methods of doing most tasks. For example, you can paint your house in many ways. Which room do you start in? Which order do you continue? What method do you use? What type of paint do you use? What is the capability of your helpers? Some of these are dictated to you whilst others are within your choice range. Investigation is often needed to help you finalize your decision. It is essential to determine the way that you are going to do the work before attempting to prepare the scope of work.

What do you think of this alternative?

In many cases there will be restrictions placed on you by management or by the circumstances. Let's look at a few of these:

- Finish as fast as possible

- Obtain best use of resources

- Obtain the cheapest cost

- Minimize equipment downtime

For example, you can complete the work quicker by adopting one or more of the following alternatives:

- Use more men

- Work shifts

- Work overtime

- Call in specialist contractors

- Use more equipment

- Do a temporary repair and risk failure

Each of these will have a direct or indirect cost implication and in many cases there will be an effect on production. For example, a production critical industry such as an oil refinery may find a higher cost option more acceptable if the effect on production is less.

In some cases the evaluation of the alternatives is an easy rapid mental process. In other cases it may be necessary to undertake detailed investigation to determine and evaluate the various alternatives.

There are always alternatives, consider the clothes that you may be wearing. How many alternatives do you have of putting them on?

It only takes basic arithmetic to produce startling results. Let's assume that we have seven pieces of clothing then we have 5,040 alternatives (7 x 6 x 5 x 4 x 3 x 2). For ten items the total soars to over three million. Of course, not every one of these alternatives is sensible, as we obviously cannot put on our socks after our shoes, etc.

Let's look at a more practical and realistic example of alternatives:

## *Example: The overhaul of motors*

A company working in an third world country has several operating bases spread out over a large area. There is an urgent need to repair 10 heavy-duty diesel engines. There are several alternative actions to be evaluated.

| OPTION | ADVANTAGES | DISADVANTAGES |
|---|---|---|
| 1. Use national workshop | • Quick turnaround | • Expensive<br>• Needs regular inspection |
| 2. Use company workshops | • Close control<br>• Cost effective | • Needs large investment<br>• Personnel problems<br>• No warranties |
| 3. Use replacement motors ex USA | • Good quality control | • Long turnaround<br>• Cash lock up high<br>• Shipping problems<br>• Complicates asset list |

This is seems to be a simple example but the reality is more complex as there are many sub options such as:

| Option 1 | Do you use local or national workshops?<br>Which workshop? |
|---|---|
| Option 2 | Do you use one central workshop?<br>Does each base do its own overhauls?<br>What about a combination of both? |

Each option and sub option needs careful consideration. In addition, it all needs to be continually reviewed, as changes will occur that may require the policy to change. For example: Import duties could be doubled which would suddenly make the USA option uneconomic.

In your routine work the problems with evaluating alternatives will be less complex but equally important.

All of these and many more are decisions that you make or are involved with. They all have cost implications and in many cases can affect downtime. Do not underestimate the importance of this evaluation process. Here are two excellent tips that work:

- **Involve others** as there is always someone that has specialist knowledge. In any case other opinions can stimulate the whole process.

- **Put your ideas down on paper** or on a whiteboard or a large sheet of paper. Use as much space as you need until you have finished.

## *Develop the work scope*

Once you have reviewed the alternatives then you must decide which of these best suits the requirements of the project or task to be done. These requirements must be clearly defined in terms of a detailed scope of work. The next part of the process is to develop the work scope by identifying the individual tasks involved, the logical order of doing the work and the estimated time and resources required. This process is basically simple.

- List activities

- Re-arrange list into a logical order

- List the resources required for each activity (estimating)

Many people find estimating to be a difficult task because it does need a commitment. Let's look at some ideas:

- Think it through yourself first, as it is surprising what you know about work that is not your specialty. This is also prepares you for the next stages.

- Involve others, particularly those who have done the work before.

- Involve those who are going to do the work as they have a direct interest in getting it right.

- Do not look for perfection. Use your common sense and if you are wrong then you change it later.

## Prepare the plan

The next stage in the process is to prepare the schedule. On very simple tasks this can be a mental process without the need for putting anything on paper. Other tasks will be more complex or there are simply too many to remember and these will need to be scheduled using some type of paper format. There are three main types of planning formats, which we will briefly discuss. Please remember that we are not going to cover planning techniques in detail but just give you the basics. These three methods are:

- Activity lists

- Bar charts

- Networks

## Activity lists

This is the simplest form of planning or scheduling. It is very useful but is very limited. However, a list of things to do is a very good starting point in getting yourself organized. Lists can be arranged and rearranged until you have all items in order of importance or in the order of work. For example, we are going to prepare a list of tasks involved in changing a wheel on a car on a highway. The list should end up looking like the following example:

**CHANGE A CAR WHEEL**
**ACTIVITY LIST**
1. Get the spare wheel
2. Get the wheel brace
3. Get the jack
4. Jack up car
5. Remove the wheel
6. Fit the spare wheel
7. Stow the removed wheel
8. Lower the car
9. Replace all the tools
10. Drive away

Why don't we create more activities?

For example, in activity 5 there are many activities such as:

1. Put wheel brace on nut 1

2. Loosen nut 1

3. Remove nut 1

4. Place nut in secure position close to work area

5. Put wheel brace on nut 2

6. Etc.

In this way we can create maybe 20 or 30 sub tasks for this action alone. Perhaps we can cover the whole operation with 150 actions, which will result in an impressive looking plan. So why don't we do this? Because:

- You are stating the obvious

- You are insulting the person that will use the plan

- It is unnecessary

There are no fixed rules on the level of detail for plans. This is usually left to individual's common sense.

---

**Important note**

You are probably thinking of how many times that you have changed a wheel without a list or a plan. Well, you are quite correct - you do such tasks using your mental planning capability. You don't even realize it because it has become automatic. The purpose of this example is to demonstrate how easy the basics of planning are.

---

## *Bar charts*

Next we will look at bar charts. These will be very useful to you if you learn to use them. First you start with the list and evaluate the needs of each activity. For example, how long will the activity take and what resources are necessary. In this case, it is obvious that one person is adequate but of course if you had a passenger with you the task of changing a wheel could be done quicker. Let's see how long the work will take using only the driver.

| ACTIVITIES | TIME NEEDED | RESOURCES |
|---|---|---|
| 1. Get spare wheel | 1 minute | 1 person |
| 2. Get wheel brace | 1 minute | 1 person |
| 3. Get jack | 1 minute | 1 person |
| 4. Jack up car | 1 minute | 1 person |
| 5. Remove wheel | 2 minutes | 1 person |
| 6. Fit spare wheel | 2 minutes | 1 person |
| 7. Stow removed wheel | 1 minute | 1 person |
| 8. Lower car | 1 minute | 1 person |
| 9. Replace tools | 2 minutes | 1 person |
| 10. Drive away | 0 minutes | |

Total time is 13 minutes. That is probably wrong and needs more thought. For in example, in the formula 1 racetracks the total operation takes around 13 seconds using sophisticated equipment. But if your grandmother was doing it in the middle of a busy motorway in heavy rain then maybe 13 minutes is not enough. So you must set the times to suit the following:

- The conditions

- The location

- The resources that you have

- The equipment that you have available

The best sources of information for assessing task durations are:

- Your experience

- People who do it regularly

- Your records of past work

- Your common sense

Did you notice that Activity 10 has 0 duration? (This is impossible if it is a task because all tasks take some time, however small it may be). This is called a **milestone**, which means that this is something that occurs in a moment of time. For example, your birthday, the end of a project, the start of the month are all milestones.

A normal bar chart simply shows in graphic form the activities to be done, the time needed and when the activities will be done.

The following example shows our wheel change again in basic bar chart format and shows time taken in minutes and you can identify the actual date the work is to be done.

| ACTIV NO | ACTIVITIES | TIMESCALE IN MINUTES | | | | | | | | | | | |
|---|---|---|---|---|---|---|---|---|---|---|---|---|---|
| | | 1 | 2 | 3 | 4 | 5 | 6 | 7 | 8 | 9 | 10 | 11 | 12 | 13 |
| 1 | Get spare wheel | ■ | | | | | | | | | | | | |
| 2 | Get wheel brace | | ■ | | | | | | | | | | | |
| 3 | Get jack | | | ■ | | | | | | | | | | |
| 4 | Jack up car | | | | ■ | | | | | | | | | |
| 5 | Remove wheel | | | | | | ■ | | | | | | | |
| 6 | Fit spare wheel | | | | | | | ■ | | | | | | |
| 7 | Stow removed wheel | | | | | | | | | ■ | | | | |
| 8 | Lower car | | | | | | | | | | ■ | | | |
| 9 | Replace tools | | | | | | | | | | | ■ | ■ | |
| 10 | Drive away | | | | | | | | | | | | | ◆ |

I ask you all. Could anything be simpler? All bar charts are basically the same although they may look different. I use them all the time at work and at home. If I have a major garden project or need to plan jobs around the house I use a bar chart. I cannot remember all the things that I have to do without this help. It also helps me to organize my thoughts.

Bar charts are very flexible and you can create your own formats that can include resources, costs or many other features.

So far we have not considered the relationships between the activities because they are so obvious that they do not need stating. But there are definite relationships - for example it is impossible to jack up the car until you have obtained a jack. In planning language it is said that activity 4 (jacking the car) is dependent on activity 3 (get the jack). In some cases an activity is dependent on more than one previous activity being completed.

## *Dependencies*

| ACTIVITY TO BE EVALUATED | DEPENDANT ACTIVITIES THAT MUST BE COMPLETED | COMMENTS |
|---|---|---|
| 1 | None | |
| 2 | None | |
| 3 | None | |
| 4 | 3 | • It is impossible to jack up the car without the jack |
| 5 | 4 and 2 | • You cannot remove the wheel until the car has been jacked up<br>• You cannot remove the wheel without the wheel brace |
| 6 | 5 and 1 | • You cannot fit the new wheel until the old one has been removed<br>• You cannot fit the new wheel until you obtain it |
| 7 | 6 | • You cannot lower the car until the new wheel is fitted |
| 8 | 6 | • You cannot lower the car until the new wheel is fitted |
| 9 | 8 | • You cannot replace the tools until you have finished with the jack |
| 10 | 8 or 9 | • As stated this is not an activity but a milestone<br>• However, it cannot happen until the work is complete<br>• Why 8 or 9? |

Think about activities 1, 2, and 3. They are essential because 6, 5 and 4 cannot start until they are finished. But when and how can they start? What do you think?

Basically they can start at anytime in the future. That is your decision or someone else's decision. If you don't need the car and can leave it where it is then you can start whenever you wish. The reality is that you will start immediately in this case.

But let's consider a different situation where your boss calls to tell you that his car has a puncture at his house and that you must change the wheel before he returns from a business trip to Buenos Aires in 3 days time. So you can start anytime up to 13 minutes before he arrives. That is a bit risky but under these circumstances you will start the work to suit your own circumstances within the time available.

- What about the order of doing 1, 2 and 3?
- Why not 3, 1 and 2 or 2, 3 and 1?
- Why not get two helpers and do all the activities at the same time?

Well you can do all these things - it is up to you to decide on the most sensible approach based on how quickly the work needs to be done, the environment, resources etc.

Do you remember our chart that said that milestone 10 (driving away) could follow 8 (lower car) or 9 (put away tools)? Why is there a choice? Well, there is nothing to stop you driving away without putting away the tools, is there? But it is a bit stupid.

## Sell the plan

We must ensure that everyone involved accepts our plan, as this is the best way to get their commitment and to create a feeling of ownership of the plan and its objectives. If you have involved people in the previous steps then you will find this final step easier to achieve.

This is our plan. What do you think?

## Be prepared to change the plan

You must be prepared to change the plan at all stages in the process. By involving others you will receive new information and suggestions that will enhance your plan. Your plan will need to be adjusted to suit the feedback of progress that will require new decisions. A plan is a dynamic document and it will always require updating.

We do not have the time available to go into more detail on the subject of network and other advanced planning methods. However, I hope that although plans can be complex the basics are simple. The key message of this chapter is that planning is fundamental to the management process and it is not difficult.

# *Action lists*

Of course, most of our work will not require the preparation of bar charts and many people do their planning in their head but there is a better way.

Maybe you have the ability to remember all your planned activities and maintain them up to date without any aides, but the rest of the human race needs to write them down. In the section on Time and Workload Management we suggested the use of an Everything Book. This book is an ideal home for your written priority list.

| THE BENEFITS OF A WRITTEN PRIORITISED ACTION LIST | |
|---|---|
| • Keeps you focused | • It's stimulating and satisfying |
| • Less memory demanding | • Visible to others |

1. List all the actions that you can think of without making judgements. That means listing small unimportant things with important complex ones. At this stage it is not important.
2. Remove the clutter by taking immediate action by identifying all the *quick and easy* to do items and do them. This may take an hour or two but it will make your next steps so much easier.
3. Evaluate the list to establish an initial priority list. The 80/20 principle will help you in this together with your knowledge of company objectives and goals. Estimate the amount of your personal time that you think will be necessary for each item. Try to complete this exercise fairly quickly; don't become too bogged down in detail at this stage. If you are not sure of something then take your best guess.
4. Rationalize the list by asking the following questions:

- Am I sure that this is my responsibility or should someone else be doing it?
- Can I delegate this? Maybe, there is someone else in your group better qualified or has more time available to do it
- Can I group some actions together and do them together?

## Networks

Up to now we have talked about our insignificant car wheel change that will get planned mentally. What about a more complex situation - for example instead of changing one wheel we are going to build a NASA space module that has hundreds of thousands of activities with countless alternatives. Now you need a plan!

When plans become larger and more complex these relationships become very important. Activities that allow us to have choices (e.g. those that can be done at the same time as 1 or more other activities) give us the power of controlling the program to meet our requirements. These projects can be done on bar charts but they become impractical. The next level of planning is to use a network (also known as PERT or CPA and many other names) which is ideally suited for computerization. These networks can look very frightening especially when you hear the new buzzwords that go with them. Do not concern yourself, as they are all based on simple concepts. The clever stuff is in the minds of the network planners not the system.

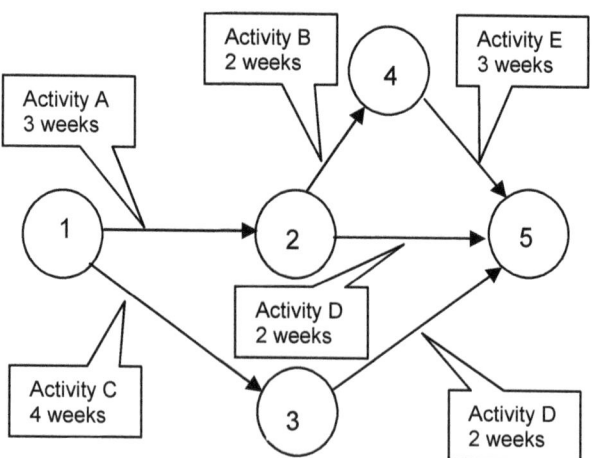

**Typical simple network diagram**

# CHAPTER 5

# HOW TO GET ORGANISED

| | |
|---|---:|
| • Introduction | 64 |
| • Organizational structure | 65 |
| • Facilities and working environment | 67 |
| • Working within the system | 67 |
| • Sources of additional resources | 69 |
| • Work standards and procedures | 70 |
| • Day to day organization | 71 |
| • Materials management | 72 |

# Introduction

## Definition

Organization is the vital step between planning the work and executing the work. Organization means the grouping and management of people, facilities and procedures that are needed to facilitate the work to be done. This management function has two main parts to it called structural organization and job organization.

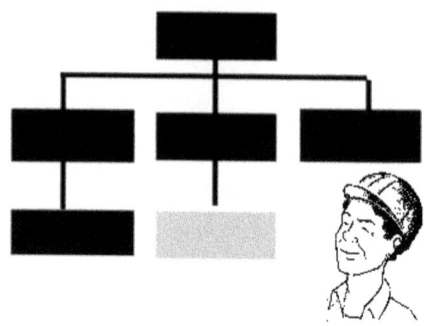

## Structural organization

This is the permanent or semi-permanent arrangement, which apply both to the company as a whole and to individual work groups. An example of structural organization would be permanent buildings such as the warehouse or other services.

Changes to this part of the organization are outside the direct control of a supervisor. However, this does not mean that you should not be of interested in this subject because you may be able to recommend changes.

| STRUCTURAL ORGANISATION IS ALL ABOUT . . . | |
|---|---|
| • The company organization structure | • Procedures |
| • Organization books | • Personnel policies |
| • Job descriptions | • Purchasing procedures |
| • Manning levels | • Buildings and facilities |
| • Technical standards | • Materials procedures and facilities |

## Job organization

This organization applies to the management of our day to day work. Without doubt this is the area which will occupy the majority of your organizational time.

| JOB ORGANISATION IS ALL ABOUT . . . | |
|---|---|
| • Evaluating work content to match people | • Ordering tools, equipment etc. |
| • Allocating people to match work | • Ordering additional resources |
| • Providing technical standards and procedures | • Co-ordination with other groups |
| • Ordering Materials | • Attending meetings |

# *Organizational structure*

## Know your organization

There are many types of organization structures in use in and these vary throughout the world and between industries. Some companies prefer strong central control whereas others decentralize. Others have created supervisor groups based on geographical areas but others have disciplined groups of say electricians only. Each type of structure has its advantages and disadvantages but in most cases we are stuck with what we have got. You may not like your structure or your position in it but it is essential that you understand clearly how it works and your line of responsibilities.

## Unofficial organizations

Every organization has a structure as described above and an unofficial organization created by the people. This is a perfectly natural phenomenon, which should be recognized but not directly encouraged. The grapevine is a product of the unofficial organization and can often provide interesting indications of the way groups feel and think. However, this information source is notoriously dangerous and should be heavily filtered.

## Organizational Tools

Nearly all companies have some documentation covering their structural organization even if it is only a scrappy chart which is wildly out of date. Other companies have very detailed documentation describing their management structure. These are often called Organizational Tools. These include organization charts, books and job descriptions.

If organizational tools exist in your company then make sure that you have a copy and that you clearly understand how they relate to you and how you relate to others.

## Supervision span

You probably inherited your group and someone else decided how many people you are responsible for. The number of subordinates that you have is often called *supervision span*. To be effective you need to keep an eye on your span level because it can easily change and you could find that the group is too big to manage effectively. Alternatively, you may find that your group matures such that it is easier to manage and you are able to supervise additional people.

| SUPERVISOR SPAN DEPENDS ON . . . | |
|---|---|
| • Volume of work to do | • Complexity and criticality of the work |
| • Geographic distribution of the work | • Maturity of the group |

## Facilities and working environment

You group are entitled to good facilities and a pleasant working environment. Workers expect basic comforts such as a place to change clothes and clean up, toilets, an eating area and shelter from the elements. We spend around 25% of our time at work so why should we accept lesser standards than we get at home. In addition, it has been proved many times that moral improves if you get these basics right.

Of course you are not responsible for the buildings and other facilities provided by the company but you do have many things that are under your control. For example, the following should be under your control:

- Cleanliness

- Good state of repair and maintenance

- Ample supply of consumables (such as toilet paper, soap etc.)

## Working within the system

As a supervisor you manage a defined part of the company. Within this area you have considerable power. It is important that you maintain your part of the company within the system.

### Maintain the line of command

Within your group you are the boss and each of your groups has line responsibility to you. You also have line responsibility to your superior. 'The integrity of this line must be protected. For example, it would be wrong if your boss by-passed

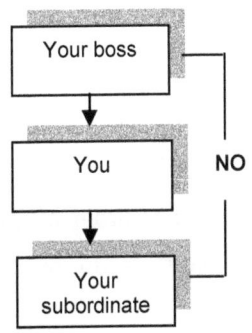

you and gave instructions directly to your group. A similar relationship between you and your boss's boss would be equally wrong. Now this does not mean that different levels of management cannot talk to each other but people with line responsibility must be very careful of such relationships when they affect the workings of the group.

## Adopt good subordinate behavior

All good leaders need to be good followers. You expect your group to follow your orders so it is not unreasonable for your boss to expect you to do the same. If you have a problem with your superior, then firstly try to see things from his point of view. If that doesn't work then talk to him and try to resolve the situation. Do not openly criticize your boss, as you will lose the respect of everyone. If you continue to have problems, which cannot be resolved, then you need to change your position in the company.

## Upward delegation

Do not be tempted to indulge in upward delegation. That is to give your boss part of your workload. It is not fair and it is not right. Of course, on times everyone has to work together to get over difficult periods but it must not become a policy. If you are having difficulty with part of your responsibilities then talk to your boss openly.

## Downward delegation

A certain amount of downward delegation of your workload can be very effective but you can never delegate the line responsibility - that is yours. Lower priority time consuming work is ideal for delegation as it allows you to concentrate on higher priority matters. Delegation if well thought out gets your group involved, which always improves morale. Never delegate final line decisions. By all means discuss these with your group, listen to their advice when that is appropriate but you must make the final decision.

## Assistants and charge-hands

It is very useful to have someone you trust and probably like to cover your position while you are not around. However, there are big dangers involved in this type of practice. For example:

- You create a barrier between yourself and your group

- You have corrupted your role. You have given a bit away.

- It looks like favoritism

- You have announced your successor

None of these will help to build confidence or team spirit. Don't do it.

## *Sources of additional or specialist resources*

Your group cannot survive without help from other groups or from other companies and organizations that provide support services.

It essential that you establish links with all outside resource groups and be aware of company procedures for their use. Typical examples of these groups would be:

- Labor supply

- Plant and equipment

- Workshops

- Maintenance help

- Specialist services

- Emergency services

## Work standards and procedures

Today's industry has become much more complicated over the years as new safety, quality and environmental controls have been introduced. This has resulted in an enormous increase in technical and administrative procedural documentation being produced. A part of your organizational duties is to be fully aware of the implications of this documentation and to ensure that your group is adequately briefed. Documentation that is required on a regular basis must be accessible to your group.

## Day to Day organization

The vast majority of the subjects above are part of the structural organization which once set up will not change much. In this part we will look at the day to day routine organization activities required for each task that we do.

| TASKS NEED |
|---|
| - People |
| - Plant and equipment |
| - Tools |
| - Materials |

| THE THREE MAIN SOURCES |
|---|
| - Within your group |
| - From another group |
| - From outside the company |

## Allocating resources

The allocation of resources that meet the requirements of the task to be done is your key organizational activity. This problem can be simplified enormously if the structural organization has been effectively set up.

As stated before, things are generally easier to manage than people are. The main exception to this rule appears to be materials, which always seem to cause disproportionate problems.

## People

Your ability to effectively allocate work to your people largely depends on your knowledge of the capability of each person in your group. This knowledge must cover both technical skills and the individual's ability to work under pressure, with minimal supervision and when maximum speed is required. Your job is to match the people with the work that you allocate. The ultimate goal will be to develop your group to a minimum acceptable standard, which will allow you to allocate the majority of work without too much discrimination. Beware of developing specialists within your group as this can reduce your flexibility and give your people soft options.

In some cases the need for outside help is obvious and compelling but it usually has cost implications. Outside help can be very helpful during peak activity times. Of course, there will always be marginal cases where you need to decide whether your group can or should do particular work. In many cases, a specialist team that does it every day can be much more effective than your own group. The decision is usually time versus cost related.

## Materials management

The activities involved in the process of materials supply are a major problem to the role of a supervisor. In chapter 1 we showed the results of an analysis of supervisor time allocations. Let's look at more figures that analyze the organization element in more detail. Once again you have the opportunity to compare your figures with the study.

| ACTIVITIES | NORMAL HOURS | OPTIMAL HOURS | YOUR HOURS |
|---|---|---|---|
| Co-ordination of materials | 5 | 10 | |
| Ordering of Materials | 10 | 1 | |
| Delivery of Materials | 12 | 0 | |
| % of supervisor's time | 27 | 15 | |

A major problem in the materials process is determining who is responsible for what. If this is not clearly established or does not work in practice then the supervisor accepts the roles of others in order to get the job done. It is clear in the following chart that supervisors become over involved in materials ordering and delivery.

This process is for illustration purposes as it depends on individual circumstances. However, in many cases, supervisors end up with nearly all the activities shown above.

## THE PROCESS

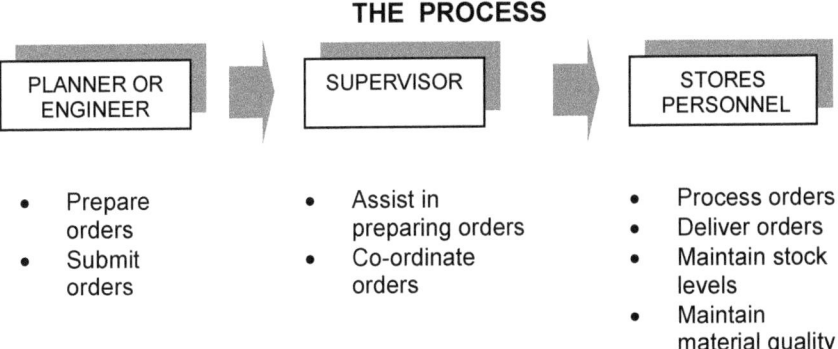

- Prepare orders
- Submit orders

- Assist in preparing orders
- Co-ordinate orders

- Process orders
- Deliver orders
- Maintain stock levels
- Maintain material quality

## Materials cost reduction programs

It is a very common practice for accountants and directors to consider the purchasing and warehouse activity to be a major opportunity for reducing costs. This policy is frequently carried out with too much enthusiasm and creates a negative effect on both production and its support activities. The two most common problems are:

- **Stock levels**

Lowering stock levels is a valid method to reduce the corporate investment required to operate the business. However, if important materials are not available when required the business can be severely damaged. There are simple formulas that the warehouse people can use to calculate the minimum and maximal level of each article in the system.

- **Quality**

Purchasing departments will often accept the risk of quality problems in the search for the cheapest product. This can result in lost production, increased costs and lost client satisfaction.

There is no doubt that sensible cost reduction and improved efficiency measures are fully justified and supervisors should support such important management initiatives.

Wherever possible, supervisors should become involved in the material processes. For example, by demonstrating the value individual items and why extra cost is justified.

Another key role of managers is to provide feed back on the effects of cost reduction and efficiency programs. If you have an example of something going wrong then record it and feed it back. This is far more effective than simply complaining.

- **Documentation**

One of the reasons that materials delays occur is simply that documentation is not correctly used. In particular, the standard of materials orders can be lamentable. Some personnel do not bother to complete all the information required or the writing is indecipherable etc. Why not look at your materials documentation to see if there is a problem within your group? If there is, then establish a training session and eliminate the problem forever.

I must get this right!

# CHAPTER 6

# CONTROL FUNCTION

| | |
|---|---:|
| • Introduction | 76 |
| • The control function in the management cycle | 76 |
| • The people factor | 77 |
| • Setting standards | 78 |
| • Measurement | 79 |
| • Putting it together | 82 |
| • The formal approach | 82 |
| • Control documents | 83 |
| • Action | 84 |

## Introduction

The word control is emotionally charged. It implies restrictions and manipulation as so vividly described by George Orwell in the book 1984.

However, in order to manage our work we have to be aware of the problems and potential problems that will affect project progress. To achieve this we need to obtain feedback information that will highlight these problems, report on progress and allow us to make changes as necessary. Information is the key element in the control loop as it initiates action.

Control is the essence of management and without it objectives, plans and all the other ideas discussed earlier are wasted.

## Control function in the management cycle

In Chapter 2 – Roles and Responsibilities we discussed the management cycle as shown below:

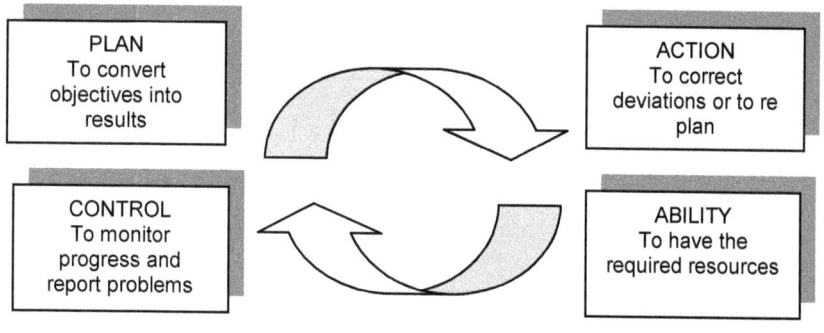

Let's look at how control works and it's benefits:

| EVALUATE | BENEFIT |
|---|---|
| HOW will we know how we are doing? | Controls will give us the feedback information for progress reports and allow us to evaluate the quality of our planning work in terms of methodology, quality, productivity and the impact on health and the environment |
| WHERE are we going? | Controls show the current trends, which can be projected to indicate their affect on the planned objectives. This is an important warning alarm that will initiate more detailed planning |
| WHERE are the opportunities and threats? | Controls identify opportunities where improvements can be made by taking opportunities or mitigating threats that have been identified by the control feedback<br><br>Control is the continuous process of adjustments (some small routine changes but others can be major) |

## *The people factor*

There are many examples of mechanical and electronic control systems. For example:

- Process control systems in refineries and other similar industries
- Mechanical governors on diesel engines
- Computer guided missiles

With management controls the essential factor is the human element which is vital to the working of any control loop. Of course we can use computers and sophisticated documents to assist us but the final success lies in human hands. We are going to discuss how to develop and use techniques to improve the human element in this process.

## Attitudes

Our first step is to address the human factor and eliminate the fear associated with control. We must demonstrate that control is positive and will help us all in succeeding with our objectives. In particular, there are two key parts of the control process that can be made more effective in human terms:

## Involvement

Your objective should be not only to involve the people working for you and alongside you but also to get their agreement on:

- Objectives
- Plans
- Actions

If people understand what is going on and the reasons for doing it, you will have gone a long way to resolving the human problem.

## Communication

Communication skills are covered in more detail a bit later in this book. You must keep your people informed. This will enforce the involvement already established. However, information must be:

- Bi-directional
- Relevant
- Simple to understand
- Useful
- Accurate
- Up to date

## *Setting standards*

Setting the appropriate standards or control levels is a key factor as it provides the benchmark to measure progress against. For machines and systems this is not too challenging as these are set by the designs, specifications and performance experience. In the case of people we are faced with the subjective problem of establishing valid standards of behavioral performance.

The most obvious way to check on the standards set is to review the feedback and undertake some detailed investigation work. However, do not immediately blame the supervisor or worker for a lack of performance. Check that you have done your part first. For example:

- Do they clearly understand the tasks
- Have they been trained
- Do they have the tools and equipment
- Etc.

## *Measurement*

It was said earlier that information must be useful. A simple message saying that everything is OK may be satisfying if it comes from a reliable source but it is not worth much more. The sender may not know all the issues involved and in any case it is only his opinion.

Almost everything can be measured

Wherever possible you need to establish some form of measuring progress. For example, if your project is to overhaul 20 pumps of the same type then you can count the number of pumps overhauled to give you fairly accurate level of progress. It is never exact as each pump will have different problems but it's a good guide. If you link numbers with time you can produce an even more effective control. For example, if your plan was to complete the 20 pumps in 10 days and you have finished 10 in 6 days then you are 1 day behind program. It is essential to have this information daily because you can now consider what action to take to recover the situation.

Let's list the actions that you could take to improve the situation:

- Maybe you can save time on another related activity

- Work overtime

- Allocate more men to the shift

- Start another shift

- Talk to operations to check the consequences

Operations may tell you that it's OK and they only need 10 and will wait for the rest. Otherwise you will need to look at the other options. You will often quickly find out that it will cost more money to recover the situation as overtime and shift work can be expensive. Of course if the work has to be completed to maintain operations it is usually worth spending the extra money but this needs to be checked out. This now introduces yet another control - money.

The important point is that if you do not have controls in place you cannot make these decisions. If you have not communicated with your people they don't know that there is a problem so there is no reason to contact you. Maybe you are very busy and forget to contact them. These situations are very common and cost companies millions of dollars.

| THE COMMON UNITS OF MEASUREMENT ARE: ||
|---|---|
| Time | e.g. downtime |
| Money | e.g. cost of spares |
| Output | e.g. meters drilled |
| Numbers | e.g. number of accidents |

Money is the ultimate measure as all the others can be converted into money, which is the final measure of a company's success or failure.

Measurement brings reality to the situation and reduces the risks of relying on opinions only. Measurement also has other spin off advantages such as:

- It forces the sender to be more accurate in his assessments.
- It improves communications by making information clear
- It makes people more disciplined in thinking through their response. They have to consider:

How many ?     How much ?     How often ?     How long ?

One significant problem with quantitative measurement is that it is not always effective. For example, how do you fully measure the human factor. When evaluating people or human oriented systems, emotional and psychological factors obviously are hard to quantify.

For example, how do you measure the psychological state of a supervisor or worker and its effect on output?

However, the difficult task of subjectively quantifying people is the most important of all control measurements and ultimately dictates the success or failure of all management systems.

## Putting it together

Management controls must be designed - they do not just appear. You cannot let it run itself by allowing people to send information when they have time or when they think it is necessary. To start with, you need to define the following:

- What information do you need?
- Where will the information come from?
- Who will provide it?
- How will it be obtained?
- How will it be presented and relayed?
- When do you want it?
- What happens to the information?

All these will change from project to project depending on size, complexity and the quality of the personnel involved. In addition, your senior management may demand specific data from time to time.

## The formal approach

These principals apply to all controls even on the smaller tasks, which are happening around you, which can be controlled mentally. On bigger tasks and where work is being done outside your direct control (at a factory, for example) then a more formal and disciplined approach will be required.

Verbal communications are excellent as they give you the opportunity of fully understanding the situation and develop solutions. However, for routine communication of information you will nearly always benefit from installing a formal paperwork system. This involves creating standard forms and procedures for recording and communication information. This has several advantages such as:

- They create good disciplines in ensuring all the information is provided correctly

- They provide a good check list reminder for the person providing the information

- People psychologically give more importance to written documents than verbal communications and this helps to ensure that timetables are met

- They provide essential records that will prove to be a good control device and provide excellent data for future analysis

## *Control documents*

You will often need to develop simple control documents that are completed and submitted as required. These will list the information that you require in a manner that others can simply fill in the information. Once set in motion these simple control documents can easily function when you are not around, as they become routine. Even if you have to be away for a few days you can delegate others to receive the incoming controls and contact you in case of your action being needed. When you return you will find a permanent record for your review.

It is worth repeating that we are establishing the fundamentals. Tasks such as an oil change may not need control documents but they do need controls even if they are performed mentally.

One of the most underused control methods is a daily dairy book that you can use to remind yourself of controls and to record actions to be taken.

## *Action*

Controls are only effective if they result in actions when needed. Later in the book we will discuss decision making and communications which will help you in taking positive action.

# CHAPTER 7

# TIME MANAGEMENT

| | |
|---|---:|
| • Introduction | 86 |
| • It's your call | 87 |
| • The five stages to success | 87 |
| • Stage 1 - Get organized | 88 |
| • Stage 2 - Analyze how you spend your time | 90 |
| • Stage 3 - Work load planning | 91 |
| • Stage 4 - Create a work load planning system | 92 |
| • Stage 5 - Eliminate notorious time wasters | 95 |
| • Some suggested solutions | 99 |
| • Sustainability | 100 |

## Introduction

Time is a precious commodity, and it should be treated as such, whether it is our time or other people's. However, a recent survey shows that over 20% of a manager's working week is wasted. This works out at an average of 1 in 5 working days being wasted. In addition, it was found that over 90 % of managers' desks and office areas were totally disorganized and around 30% of manager time was spent on routine paperwork.

This is clearly an unacceptable situation, which needs to be resolved. In a positive sense we should consider this as an opportunity to improve our production by 25%. Maybe you could work less overtime and see more of your family. Perhaps you can now control your own life. These figures may not be true for your situation but even if you could improve your available time by 10 % then that would be an impressive result.

| TIME | IN A YEAR | | LIFETIME |
|---|---|---|---|
| Time spent at work | 1,920 hours | 160 days | |
| Amount wasted using 20% | 384 hours | 32 days | 1,440 days |
| Amount wasted using 5% | 96 hours | 8 days | 360 days |

The above chart shows that the potential wasted time in your lifetime could be between 360 and 1,440 days depending on where you are on the efficiency scale. Just imagine what the value of this wasted time is.

We always talk of the lack of Time or as Time being one of our most important resources. However, we tend to blame others for wasting our time rather than ourselves. A lack of time has been a great excuse for non-performance for many years. The truth is that in the vast majority of cases, we are responsible for the use and the wastage of our time.

We cannot *make* more time; even millionaires cannot *buy* more time. The only way we can make the most of the time that we have is to plan and manage it.

This section shows how we can maximize the usage of our available hours at work and at home.

## *It's your call*

Management has a big influence on the effective use of time in an organization because they can encourage their personnel to improve time management and they can set an example to others. But as stated before we have the ability to manage our own time. Remember that, problems, tasks, telephone calls and the other time consuming activities do not organize themselves. One of the primary reasons for having a supervisor is to handle these activities. Generally we decide what we do and when we do it. Of course, we have to comply with instructions and react to situations but we always have options open to us.

## *The five stages to success*

If you accept that your time is your responsibility then I guarantee that by using the following five stages, it will result in success.

| Stage 1 | Stage 2 | Stage 3 | Stage 4 | Stage 5 |
|---|---|---|---|---|
| Get organized | Analyze how you spend your time | Work load planning | Create a workload planning system | Eliminate notorious time wasters |

## Stage 1 - Get organized

It is amazing how much time most people waste looking for documents, finding computer files, locating staplers, telephone numbers and so on. If your office is full of reference files, spare parts and miscellaneous bits and pieces then you are a magpie.

I can't find the program!

Why not come in on the weekend and organize yourself. Get a basic filing system, prepare contact lists, order the equipment that you need and organize your computer. If you don't have your own office, then organize your pick-up or get yourself a corner somewhere. This exercise will be one of the best investments that you will ever make

The first step is to review what activities you do in the office and what you need to support these activities. For example:

| THE ESSENTIALS | TAKE ACTION |
|---|---|
| TOOLS | Stapler, Hole punch, Pens, Scissors, Etc. Now go and get them! Mark up with your name and don't lose them |
| REFERENCE FILES | Very simple – list the information groups that you really need. Prepare your file name stickers and set it up. Include a general information file with personal, company and city phone lists and other data that you continually need |
| STORAGE | Once you have cleaned up the office and dumped all the accumulated rubbish then you probably have enough storage space. So don't rush off buying new storage systems until you are sure |
| THINGS | Some offices are like museums and others are like storerooms. Throw it all out unless you can fully justify keeping it |

For some of us the most difficult task is going to be throwing away our old dusty files, out of date brochures and the piles of drawings and papers that adorn our offices.

Go through every file, brochure and other clutter and ask yourself the following key questions. Please note that you must be objective and tough with yourself. YES means YES, it really must have to be of use to you and if you have doubts then make it a MAYBE:

| KEY QUESTIONS | YES | MAYBE | NO |
|---|---|---|---|
| Will I ever need this again? | | | |
| Will it be difficult to get this data from elsewhere? | | | |
| Is the information up to date? | | | |
| Was there a good reason for having it in the first place? | | | |
| Should it be with someone else? | | | |

| STATUS | ACTIONS TO BE TAKEN |
|---|---|
| YES | Organize into logic groupings and store in clearly marked files. If the information is important but rarely or never used then it should be put into long term storage systems. Only keep the information that you regularly need around you. |
| MAYBE | Have a good second thought about it and if you cannot change it to a YES then change it to a NO |
| NO | Throw it away or give it to someone else. Don't cry or delay. Think of it as losing unwanted guests. |

## Stage 2 – Analyze how you spend your time

In the earlier section on the role of a supervisor we analyzed our tasks in a general way. We now have to develop a procedure for monitoring our present time usage.

To assist in answering the above questions it is sometimes helpful to carry out your own activity monitoring,

The procedure is simple but the results can be surprising. The typical form will help you in your monitoring. It is based on a random sampling approach and will give you a good assessment of how your time disappears.

### LIFETIME ANALYSIS SHEET

NAME: _____     DATE: _____

| TIME | AT HOME | | | AT WORK | | | | |
|------|---------|---------|--------|--------|-----------|-------|----------|----------|
|      | Sleep   | At home | Social | Travel | On the job | Admin. | Meetings | Personal |
| 0700 | ✓ |   |   |   |   |   |   |   |
| 0715 |   | ✓ |   |   |   |   |   |   |
| 0730 |   |   |   | ✓ |   |   |   |   |
| 0745 |   |   |   | ✓ |   |   |   |   |
| 0800 |   |   |   |   |   | ✓ |   |   |
| 0815 |   |   |   |   |   |   | ✓ |   |
| 0830 |   |   |   |   |   |   | ✓ |   |
| 0845 |   |   |   |   |   | ✓ |   |   |
| 0900 |   |   |   |   |   | ✓ |   |   |
| 0915 |   |   |   |   |   | ✓ |   |   |
| 0930 |   |   |   |   |   | ✓ |   |   |
| 0945 |   |   |   |   |   | ✓ |   |   |
| 1000 |   |   |   |   |   |   |   | ✓ |

The basic procedures for using this form are noted below:

- Keep the form immediately to hand on your desk

- Check your activity every 15 minutes and tick the position on the chart relating to your actual activity of the given time.

- Be honest. If you are talking to a friend or on the phone to your wife it is a personal activity.

- Analyze the results and see what changes are needed. You can easily change the layout and change the column titles

## Stage 3 - Work load planning

It's that magic word again - planning. It is a good idea to think about planning your time in blocks. We established a basis for these basic blocks earlier.

Experts have suggested that the most duration for producing effective work is 90 minutes and it makes sense that we keep our daily and weekly blocks under this time limit. We can use the work we did in section 1 to assist us in developing the time block concept.

| OUR PLANNED USE OF TIME | | | |
|---|---|---|---|
| KEY ACTIVITIES | TIME % | WEEKLY TIME | TIME BLOCKS |
| Thinking | 10 | 4 hours | 4 |
| Supervising | 42 | 16.8 hours | 17 |
| Planning and controlling | 20 | 8 hours | 8 |
| Organizing | 15 | 6 hours | 6 |
| Administration | 10 | 4 hours | 4 |

| OUR PLANNED USE OF TIME ||||
|---|---|---|---|
| KEY ACTIVITIES | TIME % | WEEKLY TIME | TIME BLOCKS |
| Meetings | 3 | 1.2 hours | 1 |

Within these blocks our work comprises of two separate types of activities, which are:

- Planned activities - which we know we have to perform on a regular basis and those that we planned ahead to do.

- Unplanned activities - those that simply arise during the process of your work.

Planning has short and long term objectives. Of course we have to react to the short-term needs of today and tomorrow but we also need to plan where we are going in the future beyond tomorrow.

A good supervisor will always be thinking ahead by scheduling the next day's tasks in detail and being aware of bigger or more important tasks that are planned over a longer period. Even many of the controlled activities can be anticipated and time allowed for them in your personal schedule. This is not a difficult thing to do provided you create the time to do the forward planning. All you have to do is the following:

## Stage 4 - Create a workload planning system

To make all these ideas work you need to record things from daily plans to reminder notes. Don't use bits of paper they will inevitably get lost. Get a large page of a day diary or probably better get an A4 type robust notebook and date mark each page before you use them and follow the following four easy steps:

**Page 1** - write at the top "IMPORTANT INFORMATION" and underneath put all those bits of information that you are always forgetting. Over a year this alone will probably save you a wasted day.

**Page 2** – write at the top "DATES TO REMEMBER ". Then divide the page into 12 months or 52 weeks, as you like. In each section mark key dates such as holidays, meetings to attend, etc.

**Page 3** – write at the top "WEEK COMMENCING 1 JANUARY 2010" or whatever date you start the book on.

- Write down the time blocks to be achieved
- List your objectives for the week
- List key activities that are to be started, continued or completed
- List any specific actions that you need to do.

**Page 4** – write at the top "1 JANUARY 2010" or whatever date you start the book on. Then continue as follows:

- List all the activities that you plan to do the next day arranged in time block order
- Allocate a time against each activity including an estimated allowance for unforeseen activities (unplanned)
- Rationalize the list because you find that you cannot fit everything in or that you have spare time and you can add something

- If you have a set pattern of work already established (e.g. you visit section 45 every Wednesday) then this can be entered for the next week

- Check your daily entries with you weekly plan to ensure that you are on track

**WHY WEEKLY PLANNING?**

We live in a busy, demanding and ever changing world and it is difficult to do detailed planning much more than a week in advance. Daily planning on its own is not effective as we need more than a day to plan, organise and execute our work. Experience shows that people are happy with a week as a convenient time span. As you become more confident you can start planning in longer time spans if that proves useful.

You know that there will be change as that is the nature of our industry. It does not matter as you simply reschedule your plan. But at least you have some control established.

## Don't forget

Your planning book has many other uses and this is why some people call it an EVERYTHING book. Its use is unlimited. For example it serves as follows:

- Reminders

- Important information

- Meeting notes

- Sketches and calculations

A blank book is more flexible than a pre-prepared agenda because you choose as many pages as you wish for each day.

## Stage 5 – Eliminate notorious time wasters

There are two main types of notorious time wasters or time bandits. The first is the internal time bandits, which are the direct result of your own actions. The second type is the external time bandits, which are those imposed on you by others. External time bandits are more difficult to control but they can be mitigated successfully with a little bit of thought and effort. Let's look at these in more detail.

| INTERNAL TIME WASTERS | |
|---|---|
| Planning | This is covered earlier in the 5 stages to success but well worth repeating. This is the head time bandit |
| Procrastination | Procrastination is a wonderful word – it is also a terrible infliction that many managers suffer.<br>Procrastination occurs when we have things to do, which we don't want to do or are unsure about and they become almost permanent features in our action lists. In many cases, these are less important or even trivial matters that do not justify too much management attention. Not only do these things not get done, but also they waste an enormous amount of our time in continually thinking about not doing them. If you have this problem then the **DO IT NOW** or the **Grandma's Rule** could help you enormously. These are described later in this chapter |
| Disorganization | This is also covered earlier in the 5 stages to success. The **DO IT NOW** or the **Grandma's Rule** is also a solution for sorting out your outstanding actions and accumulated paperwork |

| EXTERNAL TIME WASTERS | |
|---|---|
| Mail | Your planning should include a time each day to go through both your paper and electronic mail. Only deal with mail once only. Throw out the junk mail immediately and sort the rest into action or file.<br>Sort out your e-mail box at least daily and avoid mixing business and personal stuff |

| EXTERNAL TIME WASTERS ||
|---|---|
| **Telephone calls** | Making telephone calls are appealing as they satisfy our desire for instant action and they can often help when opinions and clarifications are needed. However, for passing straightforward information and requests use the e-mail or fax where possible it takes less time and therefore less costly. The fax also gives you a permanent record for reference or in case of future disputes.<br>Do not get involved in long telephone calls when you are in the middle of another discussion or meeting. All you achieve is the waste of everyone's time. Politely ask if you can call back |
| **Meetings** | Meetings are one of the most scandalous areas of wasted time. In many cases you won't be in control of meetings and you will suffer in silence. Here are a few tips for your own meetings:<br>• Always plan the meeting in advance. You must know what the objectives are.<br>• Always have an agenda.<br>• Always start at the appointed time.<br>• Control the meeting. If people want to talk about non-agenda items then politely stop the conversation and suggest a discussion later.<br>• Make sure that everyone knows that there is a time limit. You may need to overrun but you are not going to let it go on forever |

| | EXTERNAL TIME WASTERS |
|---|---|
| People | One of our problems is that we want to be courteous to everyone we deal with. It is difficult to terminate conversations, as you don't wish to offend, particularly if the person involved is a friend or your boss!. This often results in you having your time wasted by having to listen to conversations that divert you from your schedule.<br>Let's look at the people problem in more detail **Visitors**<br>There are three main types of visitor which are described as follows:<br>**Casual visitors**<br>These are those visits that are social or of a general level of little immediate importance. These discussions can be useful in building relationships and gaining information from the grapevine so they are not a total waste of time. However, they can be disruptive and time wasting when you are busy or struggling with a problem.<br>The best way of dealing with this depends on the type of person and how well you know them.<br>**Work discussion**<br>Obviously urgent items are dealt with immediately. However, if you believe that the subject matter does not need an instant response and you are busy then politely listen to the visitor and take notes. Then say something such as:<br>"Can we talk about this later?" (Agree a time or call the person later to arrange the discussion)<br>When senior management calls you to ask you to meet them do you respond immediately? Most people do out of fear, subservience or curiosity. When it happens during one of your busy periods try saying:<br>"Is it all right if I can meet you in 15 min. /1 hour/2 hours etc? Unless it's urgent, of course?" |

## *Some suggested solutions*

### Instant response

It is a natural temptation to want to instantly respond to things that suddenly occur to you or as a consequence to a discussion etc. Sometimes an instant response is necessary, but in the majority of times it is not. It requires significant effort to **stop** and **think** before rushing off. If they do not need urgent attention then they should be added to your schedule at a time that suits **you**. In many cases you can later resolve a number of points at the same time.

### Learn to say NO!

One of the most important skills we can learn that will help us manage our time and maintain priorities is to say **NO** when necessary. Initially it may be difficult to do but becomes easier and easier as it becomes a behavioral habit.

Simply say in a polite way, " I'm sorry but I can't do that right now. " This usually works first time but you may have to repeat by paraphrasing, e.g. " Sorry, but it just doesn't fit into my schedule. "

This is a good example of assertive behaviour, which we cover in more detail in a later chapter.

### Be reliable

It has been recommended that you can avoid instant responses by suggesting that you call back later. This will only be effective if you do what you promise. The best way to remember a promise is to write it down even if you think you have a good memory.

## Sorting out paperwork

There are two very effective methods of avoiding procrastination and reducing the accumulating number of outstanding decisions and paperwork by getting things done! One is the ***Do it now rule*** and the other is often called the Premack principle or simply ***Grandma's law***.

| DO IT NOW RULE |
|---|
| *If it can be done now and it is reasonable to do it now then do it now* |
| The idea is that you apply self-discipline to do things once and only once and get rid of them forever. Try it as it really works. |

| GRANDMA'S LAW |
|---|
| **Grandma's law states:** *If you eat your vegetables, you can have dessert* |
| Eating vegetables for most children is a low-frequency choice whereas eating dessert is a high-frequency choice. So if you make the high-frequency choice contingent on the low-frequency choice, children will normally eat their vegetables, and with luck become to like them. At work this means that if we watch how people spend their time when they have a choice, we can identify reinforcers for them.  So all you have to do now is to list your tasks in the order of those you enjoy, onto those that you really don't want to do. Then do them one by one from the bottom of the list, that is do the unpleasant or least enjoyable tasks first. And that's where the discipline comes in. |

Do it whichever way suits you but please do it or you will never get ahead of the game.

## *Sustainability*

Starting to manage time requires us to change our behavior and become disciplined. Behavioral change is one of the most difficult to achieve, and it's easy to revert back to previous bad habits. There is no easy solution to this, as you must maintain a self-control check system.

You will need to review your performance from time to time. A typical but not exhaustive check list would be:

- What are my objectives?

- How am I spending my time?

- Is this the best use of my time?

- Is this the best approach?

As an aide to this process of sustainability you can check your progress by repeating the LifeTime Analysis exercise and see how you are doing.

> **TIME CAN BE MANAGED IF YOU ARE COMMITTED, AND OTHER PEOPLE CAN RELY ON YOUR COMMITMENTS**

# CHAPTER 8

# MAKING DECISIONS

| | | |
|---|---|---|
| • | Introduction | 102 |
| • | Dealing with simplistic decisions | 103 |
| • | Chose the right management style | 104 |
| • | Types of decisions | 105 |
| • | The rational decisive making process | 106 |
| • | Problem solving techniques | 107 |
| • | Attitude | 108 |

## Introduction

One of the world's most memorable quotes is from Shakespeare's Hamlet - **to be or not to be** is all about a decision. It was the dramatic portrait of any human being facing a critical decision, especially the final one.

Animals make decisions every waking moment of their lives, whether to run, search, fly or fight - but their decisions are mainly instinctive, based on automatic and built-in reflexes of continuous stimulus and response. Only humans have the rational capacity of reflecting on the consequences of decisions before making and executing them.

Solving problems and making decisions are at the heart of management and one of the basic functions of all managers at all levels. In this chapter, we will examine the process of problem solving and making decisions for both routine and complex situations and as an important element in the MBO (management by objectives) process.

## Decision before the decision

The first step is to undertake an initial evaluation, which is often called the decision before the decision. For example, you may find that someone has over reacted and that a decision is not really necessary. So you decide not to make a decision. Sounds obvious but so many managers miss this first step and get themselves into all sorts of unnecessary messes. Just don't use this as an excuse for inaction!

# Dealing with simplistic decisions

Simple, straightforward decisions, with little impact on others or the organization, can be made easily and efficiently. These cover the majority of day to day decisions that you make. In some cases, the decision can be almost instant but in others a brief evaluation is required before deciding. There are two common mistakes that people make in dealing with simplistic decisions, which are:

## Delay response

It's easy to delay a simple decision For example, keeping the decision under review, passing back and fore to your boss or simply leave it until it becomes forgotten or results in a crisis.

Managers that use this approach often survive but they are never respected. This type of manager is a costly liability to the organization.

Indeed, some decisions become needlessly complex simply because we delayed the action

Just as we have discussed accumulating paperwork and actions don't do this with decisions. Get rid of simplistic decisions.

## Instant decisions

This is the John Wayne style! Instant decisions maybe OK in emergencies and in insignificant decisions but they must be controlled carefully. The problems with instant decisions are:

- They use hunches in the place of rational powers

- They ignore potentially damaging side effects
- They can give the impression that all decisions have the same importance

## Choose the right management style

There are three types of management styles that you can adopt for making decisions, which are:

| Autocratic | You make the decision alone and accept full responsibility |
|---|---|
| Consultative | You shares the issue with other but you make the decision e.g. you may request help from your boss |
| Participative | You share the issues with others to generate solutions and attempt to reach agreement on a solution |

The choice of which style you adopt will depend on various factors including the following:

- The level of importance of the decision (complexity, importance and impact on the organization)
- The level of acceptability required by others in order to implement the decision
- The time available

A manager's choice of decision making styles could depend on a variety of circumstances. For example, a time restraint may need a more autocratic approach or if the decision was considered as very important then maybe a more consultative style might be required. This would allow people with appropriate knowledge and experience to be involved. If you thought that high acceptance was the most significant factor then a participative style could be selected.

## *Types of decisions*

We have discussed earlier how we dealt with low consequence simplistic decisions. We now need to address those decisions with higher levels of complexity, importance and those who have an impact on the organization as a whole.

### High consequence and complex decisions

These will need more thought before deciding on your action. You are more likely to opt for consultative decisions in high consequence job decisions. The six step approach is the solution for these decisions and is described later in this chapter.

In most cases, even complex decisions can be solved by referring to past experience or by consulting company standards, specifications and similar points of reference.

However, on occasion decisions will involve concepts that are new to you and the organization and are not covered by any known precedent. These will need the application of problem solving techniques, which are described later in this chapter.

### People orientated decisions

Don't forget that people orientated decisions (those that are directly related to people and their problems) may affect people's emotions, their disappointments, frustrations and personal aspirations. These factors must be taken into consideration when assessing how to classify a decision.

## The rational decision making process

We have already dealt with issues that don't need decisions and the day to day simplistic ones. What about more complex and important decisions? The following six step process provides a structured basis to successfully deal with these decisions.

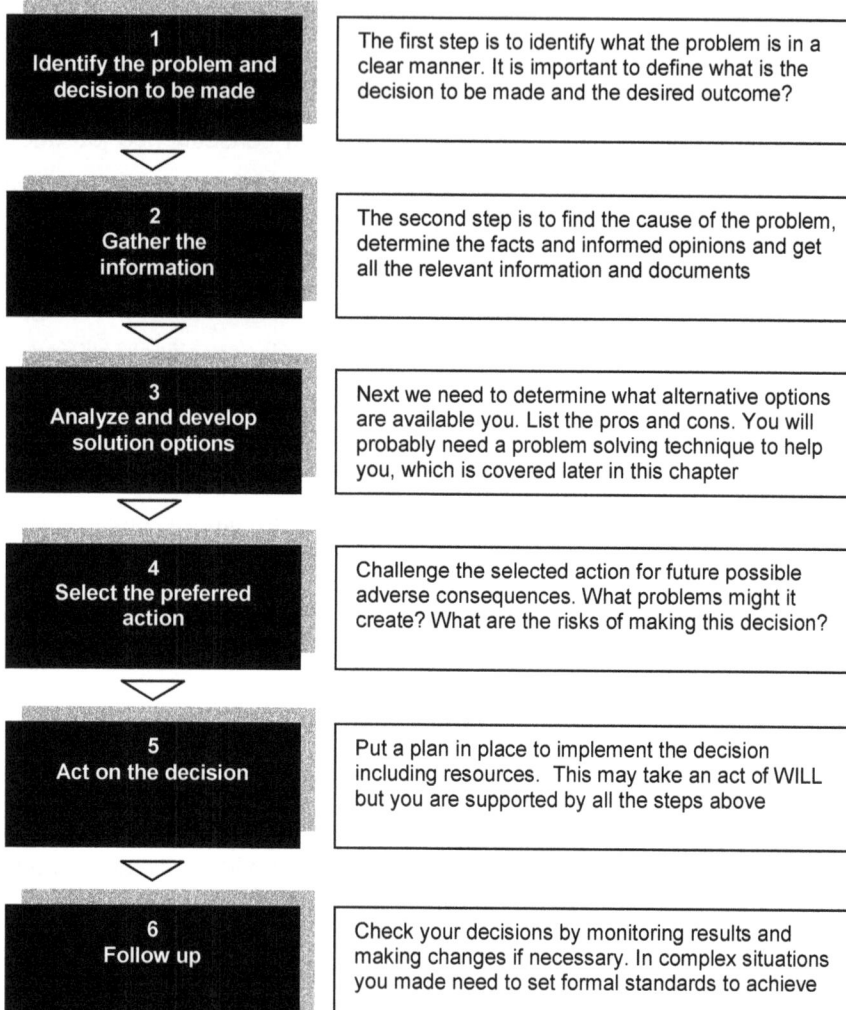

| 1<br>Identify the problem and decision to be made | The first step is to identify what the problem is in a clear manner. It is important to define what is the decision to be made and the desired outcome? |
| --- | --- |
| 2<br>Gather the information | The second step is to find the cause of the problem, determine the facts and informed opinions and get all the relevant information and documents |
| 3<br>Analyze and develop solution options | Next we need to determine what alternative options are available you. List the pros and cons. You will probably need a problem solving technique to help you, which is covered later in this chapter |
| 4<br>Select the preferred action | Challenge the selected action for future possible adverse consequences. What problems might it create? What are the risks of making this decision? |
| 5<br>Act on the decision | Put a plan in place to implement the decision including resources. This may take an act of WILL but you are supported by all the steps above |
| 6<br>Follow up | Check your decisions by monitoring results and making changes if necessary. In complex situations you made need to set formal standards to achieve |

## Problem solving techniques

There are hundreds of different problem solving techniques available. Some are extremely complex but others are simple and effective for all of us to use. One excellent simple to use method is known as brainstorming and is an ideal tool for developing creative solutions during the analysis and selection stages of the six step process covered earlier.

Brainstorming can be done by an individual alone or by assembling a group with a leader or facilitator. Individual brainstorming is a very useful tool to get your own ideas developed. However, in most cases a group is more effective as you can incorporate specialists and include those that may be impacted by the decision.

The whole idea behind brainstorming is to focus on a problem and to initially generate as many solutions as possible without any restrictions. It is common that apparently silly ideas lead to great solutions. Another reason it is so effective is that the one person's idea will often interact with other ideas with stunning results. The main brainstorming stages are:

| | |
|---|---|
| **Stage 1** | Explain to the group what problem needs to be solved and write down a brief description of the problem on whiteboard or poster to keep everyone focused |
| **Stage 2** | Write down all the solutions that are generated by the group irrespective of how silly they appear. Do NOT interpret or evaluate any ideas at this stage. After a reasonable time and all ideas have been exhausted then close the brainstorming session |
| **Stage 3** | The next stage is to analyze and rationalize the ideas into effective solutions for action |

The main role of the leader is to keep the group focused on the problem and facilitate the developing of effective practical solutions. Try it! It can be great fun and very effective.

## *Attitude*

You make decision making a lot easier and more successful if you get your attitude right. For example, try the following:

### Take a positive approach to decision making

Don't scowl or look disinterested when you are asked for a decision as that will hardly inspire confidence.

### Don't avoid decisions

If you demonstrate a negative approach to your team they may stop asking you for decisions and the results will be chaos. Always respond positively even if you are unable to give a final decision there and then.

### Make decisions!

Your team has the right to expect you to make decisions or they may stop asking you for them and this will result in chaos.

Sometimes you have to make the decision not to make a decision. At least you have made a decision and people will respect you if you have valid reasons. So use this as an effective opportunity for involving people and getting their understanding. You need to explain " why " because the decision may affect them much more than it does you.

# CHAPTER 9

# GIVING INSTRUCTIONS

| | |
|---|---:|
| • Introduction | 110 |
| • Use of authority | 110 |
| • The four key steps | 111 |
| • Don't give orders | 111 |
| • Be clear | 113 |
| • Check list for giving instructions | 114 |

## Introduction

Giving instructions is an important aspect of communications. The purpose of giving instructions is to get action. In many case, the giving of instructions will be combined with a briefing. However, in order to give effective instructions you must have the authority to do so.

## Use of authority

| THERE ARE THREE DISTINCT TYPES OF AUTHORITY . . . | |
|---|---|
| **Structural (line of authority)** | "You will do this or else. . . ." |
| **Advisory** | "You must do this if you want to resolve this problem" |
| **Personal authority** | "I would like you to this" |

With subordinates the dominant type of authority is structural. It is designed to ensure that your subordinate knows that if they do not comply then there will be consequences such as censure, discipline or in extreme cases the loss of their employment.

While talking about authority it is important that before you use authority that you are aware of your personal level of authority. Most companies have clear guidelines on this.

## The four key steps

| | |
|---|---|
| **1** Make sure you know what you want | Determine the specifics of the task you'd like completed and by when. If you're unsure about what you want, your employee will find it difficult to meet your requirements |
| **2** Give detailed instructions | Give instructions to your employee and be prepared to answers. More experienced employees will confidently ask these questions but new employees maybe nervous to ask questions to avoid looking foolish. It's your job to ensure a clear communication has been achieved |
| **3** Ensure the instruction is understood | Ask the employee to confirm that he understands what he has to do and by when. Don't accept a simple YES unless you have a high level of confidence in the person. Ask the employee to repeat back to you the information you gave or ask for feedback on your instructions |
| **4** Follow up action | It's a good idea to check in with the employee during the action period to see how he is doing and if he needs help. At the end of any significant task, it's very important to discuss the outcome with the employee. Discuss what went well and what could be improved next time. Always give praise when it's due! |

## Don't give orders

Sometimes such as in emergency situations we need to give short sharp orders. However, when you use the structural line of giving orders you may think that you appear impressive but you have a lost an opportunity. The important disadvantage of the order approach is that you have not allowed the employee any latitude for his input. He may have some good ideas of his own on what to do or how to do it. Now all they can do to is exactly what you ordered.

A much better approach is to adopt a persuasion style. The difference between persuasion and instructing is one of degree. For an important instruction that has significant impact on cost or production you should plan your approach by make your instruction as persuasive as possible. This may involve a briefing session but even with routine instructions principles still apply and they should be developed as a custom.

Why is persuasion better? Because it is far more effective! Of course you and the person or group being instructed, know that you have the executive authority to instruct them without explanation or inviting feedback. However, if the individual or group involved understand and accept the instructions you increase your chances of success for the following reasons:

- He will be more enthusiastic.

- He will use his discretion wisely in handling necessary variations.

- He will be better able to pass on the instructions to others.

People do things much better if they understand why and agree that the instructions are necessary. Think about yourselves - do you react to be told what to do without some justification. You may have to obey but isn't a bit insulting? For instance, let's look at two examples of giving the same instruction:

1. George, go to the stores and get an impact wrench

2. George, would you mind going to the stores and getting an impact wrench? We will get this job done in half the time

By using the second option it has cost you nothing except a millisecond of your time, but let's see what you have achieved:

- George has been treated with courtesy

- He knows the reason for his trip so he is less likely to get delayed

- He is now involved so if the store doesn't have the item, he's more likely to use his initiative and look elsewhere

Ask yourself - if you were George, which instruction would you prefer?

## *Be clear*

One disadvantage of the persuasion approach is that it's not as clear as an order. Orders are usually short and sharp e.g. get that job finished by Friday! That's pretty clear, I think.

When you give instructions, instead of orders, you need to be more specific and clear about the results you expect.

## Check list for giving instructions

| THE INSTRUCTION |
|---|
| - Is it necessary?<br>- Is it consistent with other instructions?<br>- How important is it to other priorities? |
| **THE RECEIVER** |
| - Who is the best person to carry this out?<br>- Has he got the ability to do it?<br>- Is he equipped with tools, materials, resources etc. to do it?<br>- Will he readily accept the responsibility? |
| **THE PRESENTATION** |
| - How much explanation of the reason is necessary?<br>- Where should the instruction be given? (e.g. in private or in front of others)<br>- What attitude should you adopt?<br>- What communication channel should you use? (e.g. talking or writing)<br>- Is the instruction clear, direct and simply worded?<br>- Has it been understood? (try asking, don't assume)<br>- Does he see any reason for failing to comply within the time required?<br>- What degree of discretion will be allowed? |
| **FOLLOW UP** |
| - When is follow up action needed?<br>- What needs to be checked?<br>- Has completion of the instruction been recognized?<br>- Is a reprimand necessary and in what form, how and where?<br>- What about a bit of praise? |

# CHAPTER 10

# ASSERTIVE BEHAVIOR

| | | |
|---|---|---|
| • | Introduction | 116 |
| • | What makes a winner or loser? | 116 |
| • | Don't underestimate your importance | 117 |
| • | It's your choice | 118 |
| • | Your style | 119 |
| • | What is behavior? | 120 |
| • | What are passive, aggressive and assertive behaviors? | 121 |
| • | Why behave assertively? | 122 |
| • | How assertive are you? | 123 |
| • | Why rights are Important | 125 |
| • | Optimizing your personal behavior | 126 |
| • | Learning to be assertive | 127 |

## Introduction

If we look again at the management cycle you will note that we need to look at communications, leadership and all the other management skills necessary to make the cycle work. Let's start by looking at ourselves and our attitudes and how we behave.

It seems logical to say that if you cannot manage yourself correctly then it is going to be extremely hard to manage others. The way that you handle yourself is an example to those around you - people need to respect you. Do not forget that it is not enough to be a nice person, respect is totally different.

The first important issue is for you to feel good about yourself – to feel like a winner and not a loser

## What makes a winner or loser?

Some people find it easy to control their lives and to realize their ambitions, while others seem doomed to failure.

Everyone can be a life winner but not everyone can release his or her potential. Most supervisors were winners otherwise they would not have been selected for such an important role. However, many supervisors have worked too long in a hostile environment without support. This is the breeding ground of the loss syndrome.

The truth is that we create our own fears and doubts. We seem to have a tape running in our head, which keeps repeating:

| It's too late | It can't be changed |
|---|---|
| You can't do it | You'll fail |
| You'll never understand | You're wasting your time |
| You're too old | Don't try |
| **JUST TURN IT OFF** ||

## *Don't underestimate your importance*

We said early that you are a winner because you had been selected for such an important role. The problem is that many supervisors have forgotten or never realized just how important their role is. Let's do a simple exercise.

| Note down the number of people that report to you |
|---|
| Every action you take has a potential effect on these people and their family's lives. You can contribute to their happiness or increase their stress levels. You can affect their income through overtime and rises. You can lose them their jobs. |

| Divide your company's turnover by the number of supervisors in the organization |
|---|
| This is a crude estimate of the amount of money that you are responsible for. Now add the cost of the facilities, equipment and other company property that you are responsible for. However you look at it, it will be a lot of money. |

You are very important and you should feel good about it!

## It's your choice

Your people want to see you working effectively, handling problems and crises in a positive manner.

| Equal | Inferior |
|---|---|
| Winner | Loser |
| Assertive | Aggressive |
| Full of hope | No hopes |
| Very happy | Not happy |

In this chapter we will look at how our basic attitudes affect our thoughts and behavior patterns. It is important to accept that we can choose to be what we want to be. The following chart is well known in the management world. It is called the OK CORRAL and was developed by Thomas Harris. The chart demonstrates the choices that we have under our own control. These choices will dictate whether we fail or succeed.

| PASSIVE | ASSERTIVE |
|---|---|
| I am not OK     =   Lose | I am OK         =   Win |
| You are OK     =   Win | You are OK   =   Win |
| I feel inadequate | I feel good about my feeling and emotions. You seem to be the same |

| PATHETIC | AGGRESSIVE |
|---|---|
| I am not OK         =   Lose | I am OK              =   Win |
| You are not OK   =   Lose | You are not OK  =   Lose |
| I feel lost and without hope the same as you | I feel aggressive most of the time |

These are the four life situations that we can adopt. You can choose which of the four psychological states that you wish to live in. These notes will assume that you are a winner and that you want to be in the **I am OK – You are OK** state. In other words, you want to be **ASSERTIVE**.

## *Your style*

Each of you is an individual and you are all different. The main thing in common is that you are all managers and you wish to improve your capabilities. You will not achieve this objective by blindly copying others. The way to success is to develop your own strengths and weaknesses using the advice given in this book.

For some reason we seem to admire strong leaders: The ones that stand their ground and take no nonsense. History shows us that so many of these *strong* leaders have ended in failure and have caused disaster in their paths. Many were arrogant and used fear and repression as their weapons. There is nothing wrong with strong leadership but it needs to be combined with management skills to be effective.

Some of you are quiet and thoughtful others noisy and prone to making quick decisions. It does not matter; you are all recognized as management potential for the future. Some of you will need to work on some skills more than others. Management is a learned skill; you are not born with it. In other words, be yourself and you will succeed.

Remember that work should be enjoyed and that a sense of humor is essential to our survival. This does not mean that you should involve yourself in silly pranks and tasteless jokes but you must be able to see the funny side of life.

## What is behavior?

Behavior is our reactions to situations and to other people. In the caveman days we developed the ability to survive by deciding when to take flight or to stay and fight. Of course, within limits, each of us would react in different ways. A more aggressive person may consider fighting where a more passive person will already be in flight. However, it is unlikely that anyone ever considered negotiating with a T Rex.

Stay and fight? Not this time!

In modern terms *flight* would represent a *passive* response and *fight* would be an *aggressive* response. Even today we respond instinctively to situations and in many cases we regret doing so. Each of us has natural levels of behavior on the aggressive / passive scale. If we act without thinking our level is obvious to see. However, in most situations we think before we act by using our past experience to help us in deciding our reaction. By introducing this thinking process we are able to control our behavior, for example, by not losing our tempers or by pretending to be angry when we are not.

Assertiveness is a controlled development of this natural skill. Let us look at the three behavior groups in more detail.

# *What are passive, aggressive and assertive behaviors?*

It has been said that behavior styles range from very aggressive to very passive. The following descriptions describe the extremes. Of course, the vast majority of people lie between the extremes, but we can all recognize somebody that seems to be living on the edges.

## Aggressive behavior

Unfortunately, people wrongly confuse assertiveness with aggression. Aggressive behavior is forcing others to agree to your view, to manipulate, to punish and blame others. Don't confuse anger with aggression as even the most passive of people can get angry.

## Passive behavior

Being passive is not showing your true feelings, always trying to please, readily accepting the blame and being anxious.

## Assertive behavior

Assertiveness is being honest, open, direct and saying what you want and expect. At the same time assertiveness means respecting others and their rights.

| **What are the differences between these different behaviors?** | | |
|---|---|---|
| 😐 **PASSIVE** | ☹ **AGGRESSIVE** | 🙂 **ASSERTIVE** |
| Behavior and attitudes profiles: | | |
| • Allows his rights to be violated.<br>• Does not achieve goals<br>• Feels frustrated, unhappy, hurt and anxious<br>• Becomes inhibited and withdrawn<br>• Allows others to choose for them<br>• Easily persuaded<br>• Accepts blame easily | • Violates the rights of others<br>• Takes advantage of others<br>• Succeeds at the expense of others<br>• Belligerent, a bully<br>• Humiliates others<br>• Explosive, unpredictable hostile and angry<br>• Forces his choices on others<br>• Stubborn | • Listens to others without interruption<br>• Show that he understands the position or opinions of others<br>• Makes own decisions based on what he thinks is right<br>• Confidently states opinions<br>• Clearly states what he wants<br>• Does not let other people intimidate him<br>• Does not damage other people |

## *Why behave assertively?*

When you behave assertively you are in control of yourself which makes it much easier to deal with situations and other people. For example assertiveness is all about the following:

### Achieving your goals quicker

Assertiveness will reduce the damaging effects of uncontrolled emotions. You can address the problems directly and get results quicker.

## Building self-confidence and self-esteem

When you stand up for yourself and begin to control your situations you are going to feel really good about it. You will notice the difference.

## Improving our ability to communicate with others

Later we will cover the importance of communication. As you will find out, assertive behavior is a key tool in improving our communication skills.

## Getting the respect of others

If you are seen to be assertive then others will notice. They will see that you will not accept nonsense and that you speak your mind. People respect these qualities.

## Increasing your popularity

Some people claim that good managers should not be popular. This is nonsense, as unnecessary unpopularity achieves nothing. One thing for sure is that nobody wants to be around a wimp or an aggressor.

## Creating personal happiness

If you achieve all this you will become happier at work and at home.

# *How assertive are you?*

The following chart is a useful guide to your level of assertiveness but it shouldn't be taken too seriously on its own. Answer each question with a circle on 1, 2 or 3 to show your response. These numbers indicate the following:

| 1 = I feel anxious | 2 = I feel OK | 3 = I feel good | | |
|---|---|---|---|---|
| **Appearance** | | | | |
| 1. Speaking in front of a group of people | | 1 | 2 | 3 |
| 2. Joining a crowd of people | | 1 | 2 | 3 |
| 3. Looking into the eyes of the people you are talking to | | 1 | 2 | 3 |
| 4. Meeting someone who you have had bad relations with | | 1 | 2 | 3 |
| **Attitude** | | | | |
| 5. Complaining about poor service | | 1 | 2 | 3 |
| 6. Asking others for their opinion of your performance | | 1 | 2 | 3 |
| 7. Asking for help | | 1 | 2 | 3 |
| 8. Give your opinion even if it is not popular | | 1 | 2 | 3 |
| **Conflict** | | | | |
| 9. Disagreeing with someone | | 1 | 2 | 3 |
| 10. Being criticized | | 1 | 2 | 3 |
| 11. Expressing opinions which differ from your boss | | 1 | 2 | 3 |
| 12. Asking someone not to smoke | | 1 | 2 | 3 |
| **Saying NO** | | | | |
| 13. When asked to work overtime (when you have justification) | | 1 | 2 | 3 |
| 14. When asked to lend money to a friend | | 1 | 2 | 3 |
| 15. When everyone else wants you to say YES | | 1 | 2 | 3 |
| 16. When asked to attend a party | | 1 | 2 | 3 |
| **Total score:** | | | | |

**Notes on score**

| | |
|---|---|
| 16 - 20 | You could dramatically improve your assertive skills |
| 21 - 30 | You are assertive on times but there is room for improvement |
| 30 – 40 | You seem to be assertive or you could be fooling yourself |
| 40 + | You are either totally dishonest or completely insensitive to the feelings of others |

# *Why rights are important*

A basic concept of Assertiveness is the idea of people having rights. Rights are important because they establish a basis of behavior that people can identify with. Once established these rights will allow us to identify and correct any violations. A fundamental of having rights is to acknowledge that these apply to others as well as yourself.

## Bill of Rights

A good way to develop the concept of rights is to create a bill of rights in the same way as countries formalized their constitution. This could be a written list, which is agreed to by a work group or a family unit. As an example this is my BILL OF RIGHTS, Yours could be different.

I have the right to:

- To ask for what I want
- To express my opinions even if they are different to those of other people
- To be listened to and taken seriously
- To say 'no'
- To disagree
- To be treated with respect
- To change my mind
- To set my own priorities
- To express emotion
- To privacy
- To be wrong
- Not to be abused or intimidated
- To make mistakes

This is my Bill of Rights. Where's yours?

## Rights and responsibilities

Rights don't exist on their own; we have to accept the responsibilities that go with them. For example if you want the right to be listened to and taken seriously, then you have to do the same for others.

For example, the last right above is: 'I have the right to make mistakes'. The responsibilities that go with this right are:

- To acknowledge a mistake and not blame others
- To put it right
- To learn from it and not continually repeat it
- To acknowledge others make mistakes

## *Optimizing your personal behavior*

You can visualize behavior as an arch, which has aggression and passiveness at each end and assertiveness at its top. You can choose your position on the arch to suit your needs at that particular moment. In other words you control the arch. Note the use of the word *choose* which signifies that you are in control.

Young children are often naturally assertive. Ask a three year old if she wants to go out and they will answer YES or NO. An adult would probably respond with a request for more information. Assertiveness is probably a lost skill that rarely occurs naturally in adults - it is a tool that you learn to use when it is required. However, it is an important and effective tool that can improve how you feel about yourself and produces results with other people. Nobody would want to be consistently assertive. You would rarely want to use assertiveness with your family and friends. In fact, there are situations when an aggressive or passive behavior is the most appropriate.

# *Learning to be assertive*

Some people are wary of behavioral changes such as assertiveness as they are afraid of changing their personality and identity. Assertive behavior has been described as a management tool, one that can be stored away when not required. It should not be over used to the extent that it affects your general behavior. Is learning to be assertive worth the effort? Well, you will not know unless you try it. Here are some basic learning steps.

## Experiment in a safe environment

You have survived many years without assertiveness so it will wait a little longer. Do not rush into it. Think of some safe situations in your life such as your family where you can practice assertiveness without worrying about the consequences.

## Set up mini projects

Identify some situations where assertive behavior would be appropriate. Plan your actions and words in advance. Try to anticipate the reaction of others and have your responses prepared. When you are ready – try it.

Be careful not to become over-assertive too quickly. You could fall into the trap of appearing arrogant if you are seen to concentrate on your rights at the expense of others. Do not rush.

## Sell the concept to others

Once you are confident using assertive behavior then you can contemplate involving others using the Bill of Rights.

## Think about assertiveness before each days actions

As a positive thinker you will be thinking of tomorrow's problems well in advance. This is a good opportunity to identify potential assertive behavior situations that will rise. Treat these as mini projects as described above. It will not be long before you are automatically moving in and out of assertive mode.

# CHAPTER 11

# LEADERSHIP AND MOTIVATION

| | |
|---|---|
| • Introduction | 130 |
| • The problem with people | 130 |
| • The hierarchy of human needs | 132 |
| • Statistic analysis | 133 |
| • What is leadership? | 135 |
| • The Holy Grail of management | 135 |
| • The tool box style | 140 |

## Introduction

> Sometimes, I think the whole world's a bit queer, except thee and me and sometimes I have my doubts about thee
>
> Two old pals in Yorkshire

There is no doubt that the single most important aspect of a supervisor's job is the management of people. Of course, the supervisor must manage resources other than people, as we discussed in the section on The Role of the Supervisor. However, none of the other resources compare in importance to PEOPLE. The challenge to manage people effectively is unquestionably the greatest of all the challenges that face all supervisors.

## The problem with people

It is estimated that there are over 6 billion human beings presently living on the planet and there are not two of these that are exactly alike. Each of us is unique. The quest to fully understand how we work has obsessed scientists and the great thinkers since the beginning of

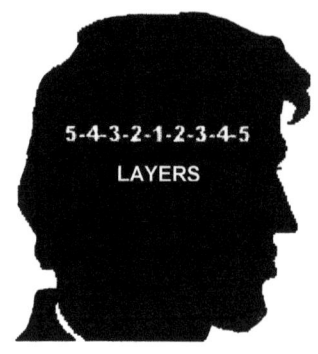

mankind. Progress has been minimal and maybe we will never know. A simplistic way for us to understand this complex issue is to consider a human as an onion with many layers. For example:

1. **Hereditary traits**

    These are our genetic strings that are passed down from generation to generation.

2. **Personal values**

   These are created when we are children and are heavily influenced by parents etc.

3. **Attitudes and beliefs**

   These are influenced by our values. It is what we think about things. For example, we may enjoy romantic music, and dislike noisy people.

4. **Feelings**

   Feelings follow attitudes. For example, when we hear romantic music then we feel good.

5. **Behavior**

   This is directly related to our feelings. For example, romantic music makes us smile, and people shouting make us angry.

One of the great challenges for the great thinkers has been to determine to what extent the features of each layer can be changed or manipulated. This has been a minefield of differing views that has created enough books to fill many warehouses. For the purposes of this book, we will assume that once someone has reached working age then he has unchangeable values, attitudes and feelings. In consequence, the only one we can work with as a manager is this final layer – our BEHAVIOR. However, we need to understand that the inner layers largely influence behavior. The final factor in our simple equation is EMOTION, which has a profound effect on our behavior. It gives us love and caring behavior but also violence and cruelty.

## The hierarchy of human needs

Mazlow and Hertzberg were two famous scientists whom developed the basic theories that established that people had structured needs and their effect on their motivation.

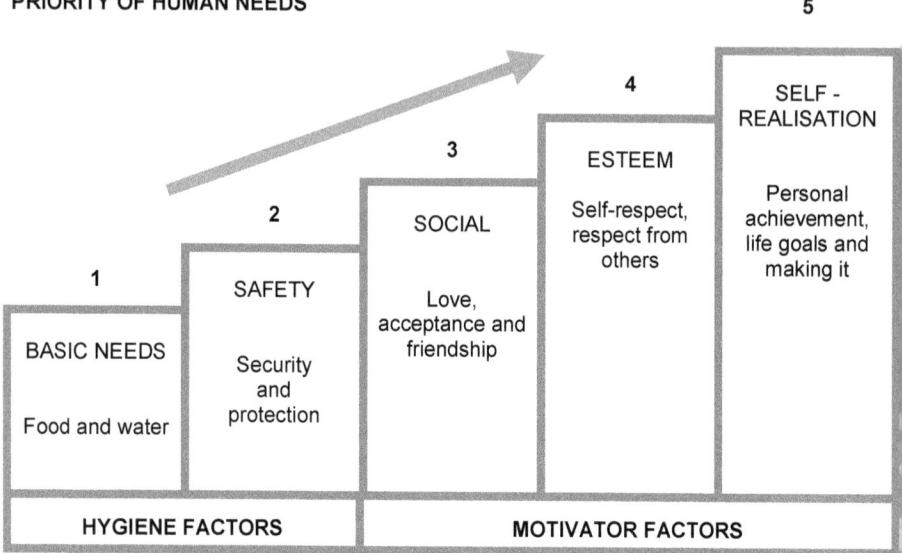

Mazlow suggested that everyone had physical and mental needs that fitted into 5 progressive groupings. In other words, needs have to be satisfied in a structured order of priority. Needs in the second group could not be satisfied until the needs of group one had been resolved.

Hertzberg simplified Mazlow's work by re-organizing the needs into two groups. The group at the lower end of the scale he called the Hygiene Factors and the higher level group was called the Motivator Factors.

## Hygiene factors

These factors now include most of the conditions that we take for granted such as housing, food, reasonable wages, safety at work, pension rights, etc. Of course, years ago our families had to fight for these rights and in some parts of the world they are still fighting. Even today, the lack of job security is a major problem in the modern industrial world. When these are satisfied it is probably a great relief but does not become an incentive for people motivation. The reason is that people consider these factors as their rights without any special feeling of wanting to improve their performance. Therefore, hygiene factors never have a positive effect but will have a negative effect if they are not satisfied. Most of the notorious authoritarian management methods used earlier in this century was based on hygiene factors.

## Motivator factors

Motivator factors have an effect, which lasts. It was found that the following were all directly job-related: responsibility, sense of achievement, recognition, interesting work, challenge and opportunity for more interesting work, even when these did not always lead to advancement. All modern management methods can be related to these motivator factors.

# *Statistic analysis*

In the '60's a lot of work was done to evaluate what really motivated workers. The responses of thousands of workers were tabulated and ranked in order of motivational influence. Not only did these studies solidly support the basic theory but also a strange phenomenon continued to reappear. Although the relative rankings were consistent, there was a typical large gap between the top six factors and all the rest.

These statistics are quite remarkable and have never been seriously contested. Of course, they have to be put into perspective and interpreted such as they can be used in a real world. For example, it is very important to realize that the above list is not based on importance, as low level motivator scorers are high potential de-motivators if not at acceptable levels. Hopefully, most societies and companies have neutralized all these de-motivators (i.e. hygiene factors) and we can concentrate on the positive aspects of motivation. However, we should always be vigilant and never take this for granted.

Another important factor is that many of the early studies and the resulting statistics concentrated on **what made people feel good** and maintained morale. This has now become more objective with more emphasis on **what motivates people to be more productive**.

# What is leadership?

It is a natural requirement of human beings, like many other animal groups, to have leaders. There are many excellent wildlife films that show the dramatic and tragic process of leadership challenges in the animal kingdom. In caveman days we probably did much the same. Although the group was not directly involved in these struggles they obviously supported the outcome. When mankind developed from being hunters to being predominantly farmers the leader role became more sophisticated and different qualities were required.

In the early days of industry we seem to have reverted back to the caveman ways with autocratic leadership based on discipline and motivated by fear. Fortunately for the majority of us this approach was eventually doomed to failure. This was partly due to the evolution of a fairer classless society but also to the work of academics that thought that there was a better way of doing things

# The Holy Grail of Management

Throughout the history of management science there has been an unrelenting quest to find a *one best leadership style*. As a result four main theories have emerged: trait theory, behavior theory, X-Y-Z theory and contingency theory. Let's review these.

At last! I have found it

## Trait theory

Around 1900 the first theorists initiated the concept that human behavior followed inner traits and that effective leadership is based on these traits which are deeply embedded in our personality. These would include intelligence, aggressiveness, physical appearance and so on, which is very consistent with the idea of natural leaders that we discussed earlier. The idea was blissfully simple: analyze the traits of all great leaders and then you can prepare a specification for the perfect leader. This approach failed because in spite of enormous research there was not one solution to be found.

## Behavior theory

The attention of the theorists turned toward *behavior* patterns to achieve their goal of the Holy Grail. Enormous studies were undertaken to classify and evaluate styles and link them to effective leadership. In the late 1960's, most of these theorists agreed that there was not one definitive style but seven, which were classified as follows:

1. Autocratic Tough (Motivates by threat and fear)

2. Autocratic Benevolent (Paternalistic, gets loyalty)

3. Bureaucratic (Rigid policies, obey the rules)

4. Diplomatic (Explain, "sell " inspire)

5. Consultative (Everyone is involved but I make the decisions)

6. Democratic (Everyone participates and the group makes decisions)

7. Free Rein (Gives subordinates full freedom)

## X - Y - Z theory

There is an interesting concept called the X-Y-Z theory, which was developed years ago by Professor McGregor. This states that there are natural management style tendencies, which are based on how we perceive people.

| THEORY X | THEORY Y |
|---|---|
| Theory X managers assume that . . .<br><br>People are basically lazy and will seek to avoid work and responsibility. They work only because the alternatives offered are not acceptable. These alternatives may be starvation, being thrown out their housing, no money for things they want to buy etc. | Theory Y managers assume that . . .<br><br>Work is as natural as any other activity and a person, given freedom and incentive, will look for responsibility and try to produce ever improving results. |
| Theory X manager's style is to. . .<br><br>• Make ALL decisions for the group<br>• Insist on total obedience<br>• Not to invite opinions or discussion<br>• To consider tasks more important than people<br>• Have limited respect for the group's capabilities | Theory Y managers style is to. .<br><br>• Invite group participation<br>• Consult the group<br>• Delegate tasks<br>• To consider people more important than tasks<br>• Have high regard for the group's capabilities |

Theory X management certainly existed in the earlier years of this century, and long before that. Many of the world's wonders such as building the pyramids were almost certainly X motivated. Managers used power and fear to motivate people. With the coming of individuals social and work rights the extreme X manager has largely become ineffective.

The Y manager certainly exists among many people such as artists, the self-employed and less obviously those who are alone and relish the social contact in work.

Another way to visualize the X-Y concept is using a scale of 1- to-10, where 1 = extreme X and 10 = extreme Y. Any management trainer or consultant with actual experience in today's workplace knows that a 10 (100% Y) workplace is idyllic and unrealistic for most industrial organizations. Thus a pure Theory Y workplace should be considered as an ideal, something to aim for but not to expect to achieve. Of course, all of us have enjoyed the Y world whenever we have had an absorbing task to do but it rarely lasts long for most of us. A more practical view is that most of us function in the middle ground by avoiding our X tendencies but always trying to improve our life situation (aiming for Y). This has been called the Z style as shown graphically below.

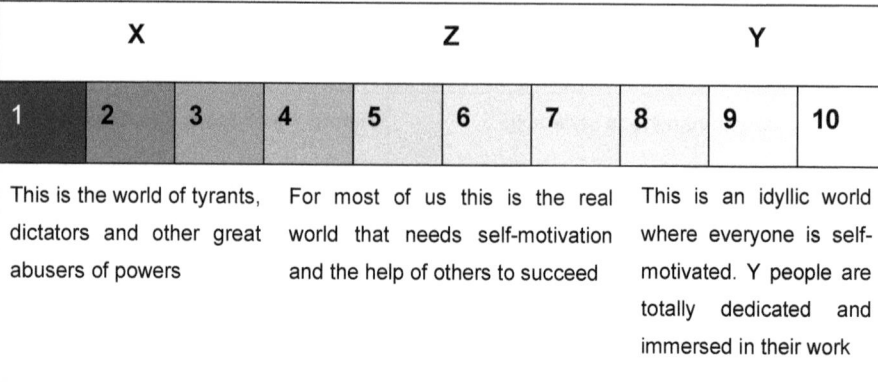

It is interesting to note the similarity between X-Y-Z and the aggression-passive-assertive human behaviors that we discussed earlier. X and Y tend to be fixed attitudes and often in our sub-conscious, whereas Z implies choice. Later we will cover toolbox leadership, which brings all these and other concepts together.

## Contingency theory

Modern management theory recognizes the value of traits and behaviors but has combined them together with other tools and thereby developed the **contingency** theory. This new approach accepted that there was no single solution and that effective managers have to use all the tools that are available to suit the various management situations that are encountered. For example, when the person or group is very inexperienced and lacking in confidence (apprentices would be in this classification) then the manager would adopt behavior style 1 which is autocratic. However, with a highly skilled and confident group he would use perhaps behavior 7, and let them get on with it. This idea was illustrated by what is known as the *continuum of leadership behavior*. It sounds complicated but it is not really as the following chart shows.

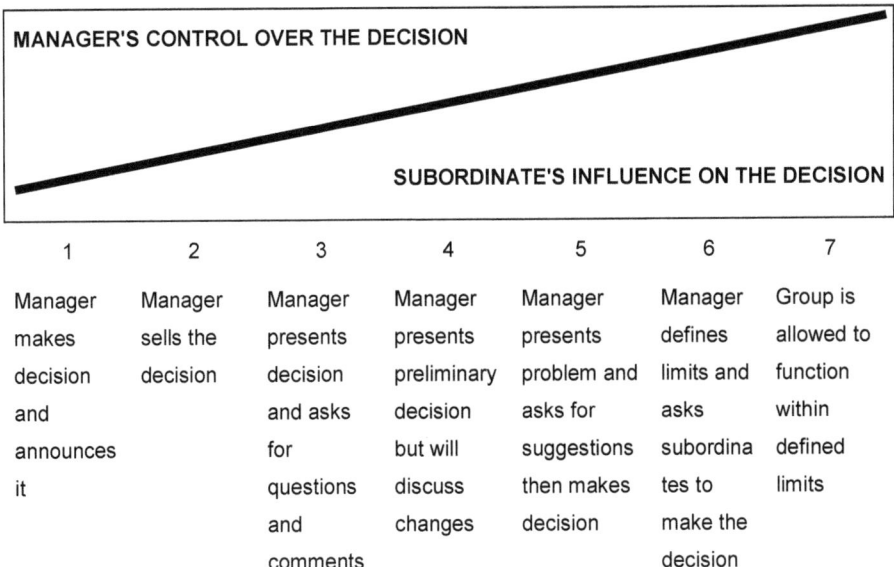

| 1 | 2 | 3 | 4 | 5 | 6 | 7 |
|---|---|---|---|---|---|---|
| Manager makes decision and announces it | Manager sells the decision | Manager presents decision and asks for questions and comments | Manager presents preliminary decision but will discuss changes | Manager presents problem and asks for suggestions then makes decision | Manager defines limits and asks subordinates to make the decision | Group is allowed to function within defined limits |

## The tool box style

Try to imagine the contingency theory like a *toolbox* where some jobs need a delicate instrument but others a heavy hammer. The choice is dictated by the job you have to do and your knowledge and skill. The tools that you have and choose and the way that you use them will determine the success of the work, and management is exactly the same. Let's look at the toolbox that you could have available if you choose to obtain them and to learn to use them. Do you remember all these?

- Aggressive-passive-assertive
- I am OK you are OK
- Manager X-Y-Z
- Behaviors 1 to 7
- Group maturity

I have all the tools I need in here

All these have one important thing in common which is that it's your choice. You don't need to be a university professor, have a degree or be a charismatic person but you do need to have the **WILL** to do it. The next chapter is designed to interpret all these ideas and theories into a practical approach that can easily be put into action.

# CHAPTER 12

# THE SCIENCE OF COMMUNICATIONS

| | |
|---|---:|
| • Introduction | 142 |
| • Why do we communicate? | 142 |
| • How communication works | 143 |
| • The communication process | 145 |
| • Coding the message | 146 |
| • Choosing the right channel | 148 |
| • Proxemics | 150 |
| • Transactional analysis | 151 |
| • Noise | 153 |
| • Sensation vs Perception vs Knowing | 154 |
| • Illusion and communication | 155 |
| • So what's the problem? | 156 |

## Introduction

Communications is at the center of the management cycle. It is needed at all stages to *oil the wheels*. It is the essential link between:

- Individuals and other individuals
- Individuals and groups of people
- Groups and other groups

Everyone is involved

We cannot read people's minds, so we must try to understand what they are communicating based on our basis senses of:

- Seeing
- Hearing
- Feeling
- Smelling
- Tasting

During this chapter we will look at the basic process of communications and some of the theories that have been developed. However, it is a vast and complex subject and we will only review the key interest areas. In following chapters we will discuss the way we can overcome communication barriers and become positive communicators.

## Why do we communicate?

This sounds a stupid question but it is more complicated than you think. All our discussions are based on the need to communicate information, give instructions and all the other reasons to help us in our work place. However there are compelling psychological and social reasons that make communication inevitable.

## The psychological function

Communication can serve two psychological functions, which are to make contact with others and to get feedback about us. We are by nature social animals, as people need other people in the same way as they need food, water and shelter. Often conversations are unimportant even trivial but they satisfy an inner need. We also communicate to maintain a good feeling about ourselves - how do we monitor ourselves, how are we doing? By communication of course!

## The social function

Communication helps us to develop and maintain relationships and to meet social obligations. When you encounter people you do not know then you have to communicate with them to get to know them. We also communicate to fulfil social obligations such as people recognition and greetings.

Can you imagine going to a bar or restaurant and not talking? In Spain they have an expression for the dinner table talking activity which is **sobre mesa**, that's how important it is to them.

# *How communication works*

Communication can be described as a process of transaction in order to create meaning or understanding between people. It is a transaction because it needs both the sender and receiver to contribute for it to be successful. Communication is the bridge between people's minds.

Effective Communication is both the science and the art of conveying information completely and without distortion from one person or a group to another.

It is a science because the principles and techniques can be learned by experience of others and by study and practice. For example:

- Children learn the meaning of words and gestures
- As we go through the education process we learn more sophisticated words
- Later in the work environment we learn technical words and expressions
- We all learn the slang and colloquialisms as they evolve

It is an art because of effect of emotion and all the options that we have to convey to convey messages. For example, the following scene takes place in the newly appointed supervisor's office:

| PERSON | REAL MESSAGE OR ATTITUDE | ACTUAL WORDS USED |
|---|---|---|
| Old employee | I need to discuss something but I don't know if he likes being interrupted | Are you busy? |
| New supervisor | I am really busy, but I don't want antagonize anyone yet. | Well, I have a lot on. How can I help you? |

These two people were adding to the science quite a proportion of art. People don't actually say what they mean or all they could. It confuses the communication process but it is an important element in human behavior.

## The communication process

We spend up to 70% of our active life communicating with one another by:

- Listening
- Reading
- Speaking
- Writing

We are going to analyze the basic process which uses up so much of our time, to see what we can learn about it. We can then see the problem areas and find solutions.

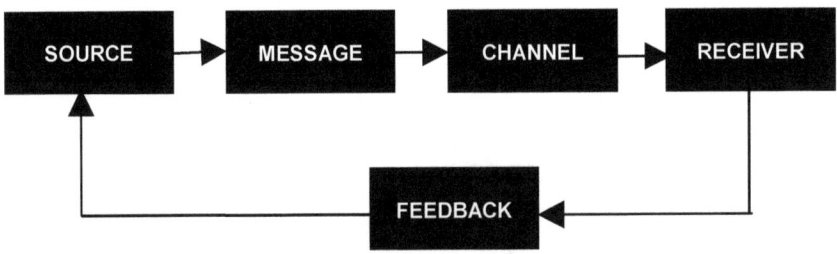

The process can be shown as follows:

The **source** and the **receiver** are the two individuals or groups that are communicating with each other. For example:

- Mohammed (**source**) is talking to his wife (**receiver**) on the telephone
- IBM (**source**) is sending a fax to their agent (**receiver**) in Cairo

The message is self explanatory but the cause of many problems, as we will see.

The channel is the method of communication as shown on the following chart:

| CHANNELS OF COMMUNICATION | |
|---|---|
| Visual | - Writing<br>- Pictures<br>- Diagrams<br>- Visual display (TV screen, etc.) |
| Audible | - Talking<br>- Listening to music etc. |

Other channels could be tactile, taste and smell. In the case of Carlos and his wife the channel is clearly **talking** and **listening**. In the case of IBM the channel is **writing.**

## *Coding the message*

In order to transmit our idea, opinion or thought to another person (receiver) we need to use some mutually acceptable and understood code. The obvious code is the verbal one, using words organized into phrases. What is not generally known is that, in face to face communications, non-verbal codes such as body language and gestures can have more impact than the verbal code. Let's look at each of these in more detail.

### Verbal

Words are symbols, which are not exact meanings; for example the word beautiful will mean something totally different to you than to someone else. Therefore by using words you cannot guarantee sending your full meaning. In addition if you use words or phrases that are not known to the receiver then a code error will occur and the transaction breaks down. People who mumble can also affect the integrity of the code particularly with similar words such as fifteen and fifty. Even words that are clearly stated can have totally different meaning impacts when the voice tone is changed. For example, saying "stop fooling around" in a soft caring tone, will change dramatically if it is said in an aggressive way.

## Non-verbal

Most non-verbal communication is unintentional and unconscious, but it can have a devastating effect. Understanding non-verbal language is essential, as some experts consider it to provide 80% to the success of effective communication. There are thousands of examples such as arms folding, clenched fists, grimaces, staring etc. A major

Body language is a key communication factor

problem with non-verbal communication is that it is often culture related, which can cause serious misunderstandings. For example, many eastern cultures avert their eyes as a mark of respect, which is easily interpreted by Westerners as a lack of confidence. In the Latin culture there is much closer contact than would be acceptable in say Northern Europe.

## Integrated

Effective communication relies on both the verbal and non-verbal messages, being consistent with each other message to avoid confusion. For example, if you ask someone if they understood what you have just said and they reply "yes" but they have glazed eyes which clearly saying "no".

The following diagram shows the integrated communication process:

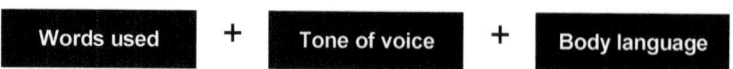

## *Choosing the right channel*

Choosing the right channel is important. For example, a supervisor who is developing a relationship with a subordinate should not do this in writing because of the need for informality and feed back. An exception to this may be policy decision, which may need to be confirmed in writing.

A contract between companies, where precision of understanding and where a permanent record is required, would not be verbal.

Talking and listening are the most important channels because they create and maintain relationships, involving people and they are creative. This is particularly true within and around our group. However, there are times when the talking channel is overused and abused. For example, if you want basic information from a vendor you are probably better off using the fax or e-mail. It is clear, recorded and you avoid the unnecessary telephone time in switchboard delays and trivial conversation. The matter of recording is very important and it is the main disadvantage of the talking channel. The writing channel is a very effective one, where having a record is important. For example:

On many occasions it is good (if not essential practice) to use the writing channel by using a note, memo or fax. This has the following benefits:

- Provided that you keep a copy then you will have a record, which you can follow up

- Records provide the essential base documentation for resolving disputes, providing evidence of action and clarifying situations
- The writing channel is normally given more importance than the talking channel. People that forget or ignore information from the talking channel are much less likely to do so with something that is documented
- They also provide a good help to our fallible memories

On many occasions you will use both channels. The written note can be supported by a discussion. This gives the advantages of both channels.

However, for our purposes we will concentrate on the talking and listening channels.

## Decoding the message

The receiver will decode the message when he receives it so that he can understand the thought behind the message.

## Feedback

This is the final part of the communication process. It has two main functions which are to confirm the validity of the sender's interpretation (to make sure he understands) and/or to expand the transaction (keep the conversation going). As we will see later this is a key part of the process of effective communication.

## Proxemics

Proxemics is all about space and how it is a communication medium. In many ways humans are similar to animals in the way they define and protect their territory in terms of the space around their homes, possessions and their personal space.

According to anthropologist Edward Hall, humans have four definable zones which affect communication as shown on the following chart:

| | HUMAN SPATIAL ZONES | | |
|---|---|---|---|
| 1. | Intimate zone | 15-46cm | This is usually restricted to family and close friends or children |
| 2. | Social zone | 1.2-3.6m | This is a zone used during parties or small gatherings |
| 3. | Personal zone | 46cm-1.2m | This is the zone we use with people we don't know very well |
| 4. | Public zone | Over 3.6m. | This zone is used by politicians, bosses when addressing a large number of people |

You can image these zones as four invisible concentric rings that surround us. The size of these will vary between cultures throughout the world. For example, Latin people are accustomed to having much closer proximity to others than northern Europeans or North Americans. Everyone can remember instances of discomfort when **strangers** enter our intimate zone, for example in congested areas such as crowded trains or in rest rooms etc. The key signs of discomfort are to avoid eye contact and to consciously avoid body contact.

## *Transactional analysis*

How many times in your life, at home and in work when you have felt really confused because a conversation has gone badly wrong. You had good intentions and you suddenly got a surprise response such as anger, disinterest, etc. Something went wrong and we normally write it off as moodiness or something similar.

It is very possible that the reason was based on the theory of TA (Transactional Analysis), originated by Eric Berne and Thomas Harris. TA provides an explanation of what can happen when it appears that you are on a different wavelength to the other person.

TA builds on the work of Sigmund Freud, who developed the concepts of the three personality states (superego, ego and Id). TA renames these states as PARENT, ADULT and CHILD, which are functioning within us throughout our lives. This is not based on chronological age or permanency. For example, we can be in one state for a few moments and then change into another, even if we are 80 years old.

TA is based on the concept that, like an iceberg, much of our personality is concealed below the water level that is in our sub-conscious. Let's look at these three states in more detail.

## The Child

The Child in you, no matter at what age, is how you felt and acted when you were a little child. Throughout your life, especially during the first five years of life, everything you saw, heard and experienced is permanently recorded in the brain and stored there until death. The child is the past and present world of feelings, needs, strivings and emotions in you. The Child, at any age, is variously angry, fun loving, loud, curious, afraid, playful, laughing, crying, self-pitying, etc. For example, the Child in us is afraid of dentists.

## The Parent

The Parent in us is the deeply ingrained memory of what our parents (and other authorities) said, did and taught us about what is *right* and *wrong*. The Parent gives us our learned value-system and conscience. The opinions of our Parent are received, usually without question, views including religious conviction, bias and prejudice, moral beliefs and a whole range of *do's* and *don'ts*.

## The adult

The **adult** in us is the rational part of us, our center of logic, intelligence and thought. It makes us realists and problem-solvers. Whereas the **child** is the natural elemental force of emotion and feeling within us and the **parent** is the strong believer in rules and standards learned from others (a taught concept of life), our **adult** learns from its own experiences. The adult is in the real world, analyses real-life happenings and information and use this thought process to override validity and practicality of **parent** opinions and **child** desires, when necessary.

In practice when we are under pressure or simply tired our **adult** state can easily be over ridden by the sub-conscious states and this often results in irrational, incomplete or emotional messages being sent. If the receiver is also outside the **adult** stage then effective conversation can become difficult and potentially damaging. The main problem shown by TA is when crossed transactions occur. Let's look at two examples of this between a husband and his wife.

**Example 1**

He says - What a day in the office! I have a terrible headache. She replies - You have a headache. What about me? Ten hours in this house with your kids is driving me crazy.

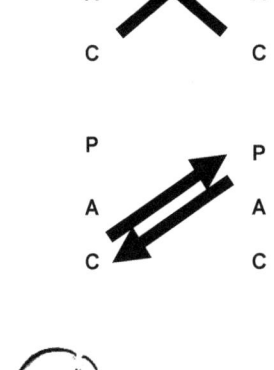

**Example 2**

He says - What a day in the office! I have a terrible headache. She says – She replies – Me too. I'll get you a cool drink and we can relax.

In the first example both the husband and wife are coming from the **child to parent** direction which causes a cross transaction. It is not difficult to imagine how this conversation could develop towards an argument or at least disappointment between the couple. In contrast, the second example shows how the wife responds in the **parent – child** direction and empathizes with her husband.

I am not suggesting that in addition to being a supervisor you have to be a psychologist too but if you understand the problem then you are half way to dealing with it.

## *Noise*

The effectiveness of communication can be reduced considerably by what is called **noise**. Noise is any stimulus that gets in the way of the communication transaction and can be external noise (such as a machine running) or mental noise (such as daydreaming).

## External Noise

External noises are the sights, sounds, thoughts and other distractions that reduce your ability to concentrate on the intended meaning. It could be general background noise in a busy factory or a sudden noise that startles you.

## Internal noise

How many times have you been preoccupied with other thoughts and not listening fully to what someone was trying to tell you? Perhaps you were thinking of the last conversation that you had or what you are going to do next. This is internal noise.

# *Sensation vs Perception vs Knowing*

These three functions of the human mind are completely different, but are commonly treated as the same things, control every human's perception or "knowledge" of the world and affect all daily communications within it.

**Sensation** is the act of any of our five senses such as *seeing* a shape, *hearing* a noise, *touching* a tree, *smelling* perfume or *tasting* an apple. We are being bombarded by millions of these sensations every second of our lives. They are received automatically and unconsciously, even when we are asleep. They are stored (as images) and recalled by the brain's memory.

**Perception** is an instant, automatic and subconscious series of mental activities that processes our sensations so rapidly as to seem part of sensation itself. Our perception determines what sense data to pay attention to and how we then organize it. Perception is like an interaction between sensations and our memory and developed further by our imagination. The result is that each of us perceives an identical scene differently based on our inherent interests, goals and past experiences.

For example, a landscape painter and a homebuilder, both looking at the same land site and clump of trees, perceive it totally differently. The painter "sees" only colors, shadows and artistic shapes, the builder only inclines for water drainage and trees to be cut down. As a result so called reality is not one definable thing but what the individual perceives it to be.

**Knowing** (knowledge) is the firm mental convictions about what is true or false, based on mental analysis of our sense data and perceptions - or by faith. Knowledge is very flawed as we can see from centuries of searching for the truth. Each technological development challenges our understanding of knowledge. When knowledge fails us then we turn to faith.

## *Illusion and communication*

Magicians earn money by openly and honestly "tricking" our senses. It's an honest game people enjoy, laughing at their mental frailty but generally does no harm. For example, look at this picture of a woman or is it two women? Which did you see first? Or which did you want to see first?

Scientists now know that matter exists totally differently than our grandfathers would have perceived it. It is mainly empty space, with tiny and huge particles linked by invisible energy. This is almost a microcosm of the universe of suns and planets separated by billions of miles of empty space. When you look at an object you perceive it as hard, solid matter but in reality most of it is empty space. But is it the truth? Maybe today's truths will become tomorrow's illusions or merely our perceptions, not reality at all.

The lesson for us is always to be cautious about communicated perceived **facts** and **knowledge.**

## So what's the problem?

Up to now it all seems fairly straight forward but in reality there are so many barriers to good communication that it is amazing that we manage it all. Unfortunately in many cases we don't and there are many famous or infamous cases of disastrous communication.

A wonderful but tragic example of poor management and diabolical communications was the Charge of the Light Brigade immortalized by Tennyson's famous poem. On the October 25, 1854, six hundred and seventy three men died as a result of a cavalry charge down the wrong valley to attack the wrong target.

Another example is that during the first month of the Gulf war in 1991 there were more Americans killed by *friendly* fire than by the enemy, which was a direct result of poor communications. History is littered with such examples.

Let's look at some of the problems by reviewing the external barriers to effective communications:

| Type of barriers | Negative effects |
|---|---|
| Psychological | **Emotions**<br><br>Your emotions could be a barrier to communication if you are engrossed in your emotions for some reason. In such cases, you tend to have trouble listening to others or understanding the message conveyed to you. A few of the emotional interferences include hostility, anger, resentfulness and fear<br><br>**Stress**<br><br>One of the major communication barriers faced by employees in today's world is stress. People under stress may find it difficult to understand the message, which creates serious communication problems.<br><br>**Prejudice**<br><br>This is one of the hardest barriers to overcome as people rarely admit to it. Prejudice can relate to age, gender, education and cultural differences that separate people and complicates communications channels |
| Physical | One of the major barriers of communication is the physical barrier such as separated working areas, poor lighting, out of date equipment, background noise, etc. |
| Language | This is probably the greatest barrier to effective communication. If the people talking and listening do not have similar command of the language then the message is under threat. For example, problems occur between people when one or more is talking outside their native language or where dialects and heavy accents are involved. Add to this the continual changes being made to language by young people; you have a huge potential set of barriers |
| Lack of Subject Knowledge | If a person who sends a message lacks subject knowledge then he may not be able to convey his message clearly. The receiver could misunderstand his message, and this could lead to a barrier to effective communication |

## Behavioral barriers

As you can see there is a mountain of barriers in your way even before a single word is spoken! Let's now look at the addition barriers that we add to the problem due to our individual behavior.

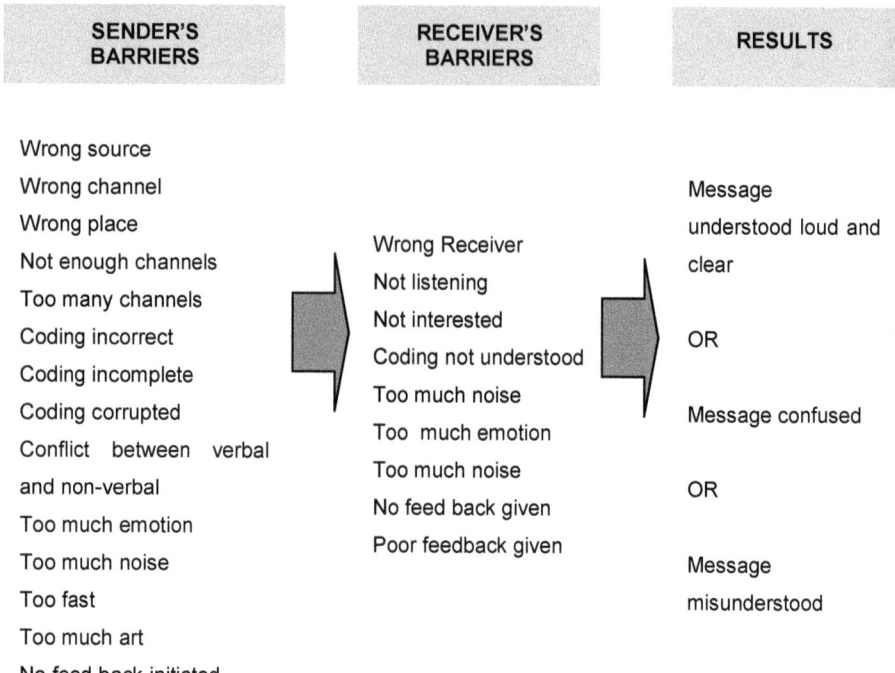

| SENDER'S BARRIERS | RECEIVER'S BARRIERS | RESULTS |
|---|---|---|
| Wrong source | | |
| Wrong channel | | Message understood loud and clear |
| Wrong place | Wrong Receiver | |
| Not enough channels | Not listening | |
| Too many channels | Not interested | |
| Coding incorrect | Coding not understood | OR |
| Coding incomplete | Too much noise | |
| Coding corrupted | Too much emotion | Message confused |
| Conflict between verbal and non-verbal | Too much noise | |
| Too much emotion | No feed back given | OR |
| Too much noise | Poor feedback given | |
| Too fast | | Message misunderstood |
| Too much art | | |
| No feed back initiated | | |

This list is in no way exhaustive and I am sure that you can add many more barriers but it does highlight the problem. In the next chapter on Effective Communication we will discuss how to overcome these barriers and to use easy techniques to dramatically improve our communication skills.

# CHAPTER 13

# EFFECTIVE COMMUNICATION

| | | |
|---|---|---|
| • | Introduction | 160 |
| • | Talking | 162 |
| • | Listening | 164 |
| • | Active listening | 166 |
| • | Feed back | 167 |
| • | Creativity and communications | 170 |
| • | Gearing | 173 |

## Introduction

In the previous chapter we discussed the science of communication and the barriers to effective communication. In particular, we briefly covered some of the key scientific theories in order to demonstrate the complexity of the subject. Nobody expects a manager to become a psychologist and a philosopher in addition to all the other demanding duties but it is important to be aware of the problems and their reasons. We are now going to consider the practical problems (barriers) of communication and the effective solutions. In contrast to the complexity of the last chapter we will see how easy it is to improve our inter-personal communication skills by using and developing methods that anyone can master. First, let's look at the four key factors involved in inter personal communication and later we will consider some of the positive solutions.

### 1. Complacency

The first and most deadly **sin** in the communication process is **complacency**. A common failure that all of us seem to have, is thinking that we communicate well and it's always the other persons fault when it goes wrong. The truth is hardly anyone communicates well all the time whereas others never seem to get it right but we never do anything about it. Remember that as a manager **YOU** are responsible for the success of communicating with your subordinates and not the other way round.

Somebody is not with us!

### 2. Lack of concentration

Concentration is the second biggest **sin**. We know that communication is a complex process with many barriers and thousands of combinations of barriers. Without concentration you will not communicate effectively so make a conscious effort to concentrate. There are none so deaf as those who do not want to hear.

## 3. Lack of interest and care

This technically often referred to as empathy with the other person. Put yourself in the other person's shoes and consider his feelings and problems. Maintain eye contact, make encouraging responses, and adopt positive body language. Remember that the person or people that you are talking to may have emotional problems with the information

Maintain good eye contact!

and the changes that may be involved and this is a serious barrier. We discuss this in more detail in the chapter 18 (Action for Success).

You don't need a degree in psychology to do all this, only the will to do it. Put these three into practice and you will be amazed at the difference. Now we are going to look at the practical things that you can do to improve the process further.

## 4. No feedback

It is obvious that feedback is important if you are asking for information but it is almost equally important in all other communications. The only way that you know if the message has been correctly received is by feedback. Much of this feedback is body language such as glazed eyes or facial expressions. This is such an important subject that we will deal with it in much more detail later in this chapter.

## *Talking*

Let's look in more detail at the reasons we need to talk within the work environment. There are four main categories.

### Social

Do not under estimate the importance of the need to communicate socially. This is covered in the chapters on leadership and motivation. Social chats can often be an excellent source of good information in addition to their contribution to personal and group harmony.

### Give information

Giving information is also called briefing and it is the process of passing on knowledge, feelings and opinions. The importance of briefing is directly relative to the importance and complexity of the message but even simple social statements can cause serious problems if not done well. Let's look at ways of getting it right.

### Get the code right

People can only understand you if you are using a code that they recognize and understand. For example:

- Keep it as simple as possible and avoid jargon or sophisticated language. It may seem clever but you will fail to communicate your message and in addition you will probably embarrass the other person and lose his respect.

- Make it complete. Statements that are just exclamations or are not finished are open to artistic interpretation.

- Say what you mean and mean what you say. Don't use riddles be straight o the point.

## Memory

Don't overload people's memories or the message will not be received fully and certainly not remembered. This is very important when giving briefings on company policy, work instructions and similar subjects. The following will help you in this:

- Group information and number groups. For example, if you have three main points then treat them in order 1, 2 and 3. People will remember that there were three points and that will help them recall the entire message.

- It has been said that human memory is limited to seven groups of information and that five groups are the easiest to remember. You will need to take notes if more than seven points are involved.

- Keep it structured. Wherever possible one point should lead to another.

## To get information

We cannot always rely on others to give us the information that we need for many reasons. Maybe they don't know we need it or we don't know that they have it. In any case, we need to talk to others in such a way as to extract this information by using questions that provide good feedback. We will cover this a little later in this chapter.

## To give instructions

Giving instructions is an important aspect of communications. The purpose of giving instructions is to get action. In many cases, the giving of instructions will be combined with a briefing and the same methods apply. However, in order to give effective instructions you must have the authority to do so and this is discussed in the *leadership* chapter.

## *Listening*

Up to now, we have concentrated on giving orders and passing information. However, effective communication is a process of two directions, this means that we have to listen as well as talk. Listening will provide us with essential feedback.

Of all the barriers to effective communication poor listening is the most damaging. Unfortunately, it is also the part of the process that most of us do worst. The problem is nearly always complacency when listening and a lack of conscious concentration. Of the four basic communication functions, we tend to concentrate well on speaking and writing, fairly well on reading but we concentrate little on listening.

We have two ears but only one mouth. What does that tell us?

Most people who think that they are listening are in fact preparing their response, interrupting, daydreaming, etc. A person with message to give or a problem needs to be listened to. The problem is that in reality our conversations are double monologues. Person B is waiting for person A to pause so that he can start talking.

Effective listening is focused on the other person. Communication is not simply an opportunity for everyone to talk. Good communication will help everyone to be independent and mature thinkers.

## Lack of responsibility

The underlying reason for this is simple in that we are not doing it ourselves. When we talk then we have to take direct responsibility for what we say because we do not want to give a poor image of ourselves or say something that could hurt us in the future. This does not mean that we are necessarily good at talking, but it does focus our attention. However, when we listen we have no direct responsibility, as the other person is taking all the risks, so we can relax or even worse **turn off**. Listening seems to require no effort as it's easy to appear alert, but in reality be half-asleep and only hearing sounds but not listening to the message. Even more dangerous than not listening at all is half listening (understanding only parts of a message) which, combined with all the barriers discussed above will end up with assumptions and artistic interpretations, etc.

## Speed and concentration

Another reason is that we are able to think at a much faster rate than we can talk. It is estimated that the average person can process around 500 words a minute but we talk at around 250 words a minute, so it becomes easy for the mind to wander if you do not seriously concentrate.

## Common errors

The commonest mistakes that are made when we should be listening are:

1. To assume that we should resolve the problem for the person who is talking

2. To say what we would do under these circumstances

3. To try to reduce the importance of the subject, for example by saying: "Oh, it is not as bad as you are saying. I remember once that . . . "

The person that has a problem does not necessarily want your solutions, neither do they want you to tell them that their problem is not important or that you have had worst problems. Some people will accept your advice as it is an easy option (and they now have somebody to blame if it all goes wrong). These people will never learn or develop their personal skills.

What people need is your help so that they can find their own solutions to problems. Your basic role is to be quiet and interested in what is being said. This may appear to be a passive activity but it requires a high level of active concentration.

Try to say as little as possible other than to encourage or confirm your understanding. For example, a grunt or a nod of the head are often enough to keep the conversation going. Don't judge, criticize or insist on giving advice.

For managers, non-listening or half listening is a route to failure, since most of the information we use to make vital decisions comes through our ears. We get (or miss) this information based on how well we listen for it. The lack of critically needed information, distortions and misunderstandings cause many communication disasters. The solution is very simple and is called *Active Listening*.

## *Active Listening*

Let's look at the rules to be an active listener:

### Concentrate

Clear away all your internal thoughts and work hard at it, concentrate intensely on every word spoken and the speaker's body movements and gestures, listen to the real message. A very common fault is to jump to conclusions or to pre-determine your response before the message has been completed. It is easy to spot someone who is not listening, because they avoid eye contact and fidget with papers or other things. This is not only a lack of respect, but also a clear message that says, "I am not interested in what you are saying."

## Show interest

You can improve the process considerably by empathizing with the other person. Try nodding now and again; use mmm type noises to show that you are interested. However, this must be done in a genuine manner not sarcastically or out of boredom.

## Give time

Good communication needs time, be patient and let the person express himself.

## Do not interrupt

This is a terrible failing in the listening process. Your turn will come so let the other finish first. The only justifiable time to intervene is when someone has lost his way or is stuck for words, then you can prompt him back on track, and you continue to listen. NEVER interrupt to disagree or impose your opinion on him.

Active listening is more an act of will than a skill to be learned. If **YOU** decide to do it then you can, anyone can, and it will work.

# *Feed back*

The importance of feed back cannot be over-stated and is a critical element in effective communication. The most important contribution of feed back is that it allows us to verify if our messages have been received correctly.

## Sender feedback

Feed back is particularly effective in face to face briefing or giving instructions where you can get the essential body language feed back. In many cases, people don't like to admit that they do not understand so how can you assure yourselves that the message has been received correctly? The following will help:

- **Ask!**

We are often too busy to get on with other things that we don't ask people if they understand. It is all assumed. How many times have you seen someone rush in and say something and rush off again without waiting for a response? To be effective the asking process must be done in a way that is not aggressive or embarrassing to others. For example:

Is that OK, Carlos? – I hope that I have expressed myself well and that you understand – Do you want me to run through that again? – Any questions?

It is so easy, so why not do it whenever you have something important to say?

- **Check body language**

We stated earlier that up to 80% of face to face communication is about body language. We have all experienced conversation where someone says "yes" but the body is saying "no" or "I am not sure." Children give us wonderful examples of this type of behavior, as they are so open with their body language.

## Receiver feedback

Feed back is also a powerful method of checking that you have received the message correctly. It is possible that the sender failed to overcome his barriers or it may be a result of yours, or both. Let's look at what we can do.

- **Repetition**

Why not politely ask the person to say it again? For example:

I am sorry but I am not sure I got all that. Do you mind saying it again?

- **Reflective response**

This is a really good way to make sure that you are on the same wavelength as the other person. You re-state in your own words what you think the message is. This has two advantages as it allows you to check if you have got the correct message but you also give the other person the opportunity to elaborate. For example:

He thinks: I am not happy with the tools that have been provided and he says: "There must be a better way getting this job done, it is taking too long."

You think: He is unhappy with the procedure and says reflectively: "That's interesting; you seem to be saying that we need to review the work method."

He responds: "Well that would be useful too, but our main problem is the quality and range of the tools."

In this simple conversation the reflective response enabled you to get the real meaning of the message and to learn about two problems that exist.

Try and stay as near as possible to a restatement of what the other person has said.

Reflective statements can also help when someone is having difficulty in expressing himself. You can summarize what the other person has said, without adding your own opinion. This not only helps to clarify the message but also gets the other person back on track.

It is important when using reflective statements to encourage the other person and not to put him on the defensive.

## *Creativity and communications*

Up to now we have restricted our thoughts to the process of communications and overcoming the basic barriers but there is much more than that. Using, and abusing, effective communications in a creative way has been elevated to almost an art form by many lawyers, salesmen and politicians all over the world. Many of these people are charismatic or very clever, but the communication methods that they use are available to all of us. For example, some heavy pressure selling companies prefer to employ compliant people that follow their rules and do not think for themselves. These companies have developed step by step communication procedures that are designed to get feed back, which they can *use* to achieve their sales. As a result many people end up buying things they don't want. On a more positive note reputable investigative journalists, detectives and others use this creativity to get the information that they require. These methods can easily be learned and practiced and they really work.

As managers we need information continually to help us make good decisions and to develop our knowledge banks for forming opinions, etc. The amount of knowledge that is available is almost infinite if we know how to tap it. In most cases we are looking for specific information for a work activity or some project. For example, as we discussed earlier, good planning requires us to get the facts, which are not always forthcoming from the *simple* communication process. The obvious solution is to ask questions but creativity is all about asking the right questions. We have already discussed reflective responses let's look at some more powerful tools that we can use.

## Positive responses

In many cases blocks in conversations occur. This is often due to the talker losing their way or having difficulty in expressing himself or herself. A positive response is an excellent method of providing assistance to the communication process. You could inspire the other person by asking a question that encourages profound thought. For example:

What do you think the main problem is?

>   **What do you see as the main problem?**

>   **What do you want to achieve?**

Another positive response would be to challenge the other person's line of thought without putting an alternative yourself.

>   **What type of reaction do you think that you will get?**

Sometimes a person's feelings may be a barrier and it can be useful to invite the person to share their feelings with you. You could say something like:

**How do you feel about this problem?**

**Why are you so tense about this?**

However you must take great care when other people's feelings are involved and it is vital that you avoid judging them. Feelings don't have morality, they are not correct or incorrect, they simply are. It is only what we do as a result of our feelings that involves morality. You could say something like:

**I can understand why you're feeling like that**

If somebody remains quiet then this does not automatically mean that they need prompting, perhaps they are thinking. Don't forget that pauses always seem longer to the person that is listening. It is important to control the normal human dislike of conversational silence when the other person is spending a long time in thinking out the situation. Just wait and show interest.

## Closed questions

When you need a firm answer such as a clear YES or NO then closed questions are valuable. Closed questions normally have a pronoun as the second word such as:

Do you...?    Have they.... ?    Can I...?    Will you ... ?.

However, closed questions are not effective in getting new information.

## Open Questions

Open questions are ones to which the other person cannot simply reply with 'Yes' or 'No', which is very useful for both getting information and encouraging the other person to speak more deeply about the subject.

Watch any successful television interviewer, except one who is trying to provoke the other person into making a disclosure of some sort, and you will see that most of the questions start with the same six words.

WHAT - WHEN - WHERE - HOW - WHO - WHY

## *Gearing*

You use open questions to get information flowing but this needs to be done in a structured way. If you start off with a difficult question you can often stop the process without achieving anything. It's a bit like driving your car through the gears; you start in first and slowly move up to four or five. For this reason this process is called *gearing*.

### First gear

WHO, WHAT, WHEN AND WHERE are first gear questions. They are usually easy for the other person to deal with, as the answers are usually simply facts.

### Second gear

HOW questions are normally demanding because they need more commitment and need to be expressed correctly. This is a sort of intermediate gear and it is not a good way to get the conversation started.

### Third gear

WHY asks the other person to justify something. Questions starting with WHY are top gear and should be left until the conversation is going well.

These are general rules and they don't always apply and even the Who, What, When and Where questions can be challenging. As a rule of thumb you will get discussion or conversation flowing best by asking initial questions that require short answers.

Of course, much of the success of this type of questioning depends on the responses that you can get and you may need to rephrase questions and slowly move towards your objective. Politicians for example rarely answer the questions they are given and the interviewer has to continually return to the same question until he just gives up!

## Some examples of open questions are:

- What do you do next?
- Where do you keep ....?
- When do you.......?
- Who is responsible for......?
- Who knows how to .... ?
- What do you mean when?
- What sort of reaction do you think that would get?
- What do you hope to achieve by that?
- What other things should you consider?
- What else can you say about that?
- What other alternatives are there?
- How can you persuade them to go along with the idea?
- Why do you think that?
- Why do you think that happened?
- Why do you say that?
- What does that mean to you?

Nobody is suggesting that **every time** you are in a discussion you have to go through a complex thought process first. Use these methods for important conversations and the more you practice them then you will find that they become natural to you. Try them.

# CHAPTER 14

# COUNSELING AND TRAINING

| | | |
|---|---|---|
| • | Introduction | 176 |
| • | Counseling | 178 |
| • | Preparation | 180 |
| • | Choose the approach | 181 |
| • | The six steps | 182 |
| • | On the job training | 184 |
| • | Don't be a schoolteacher | 186 |
| • | The three areas for on the job training | 186 |
| • | Get prepared | 187 |
| • | The four step Process | 190 |

## Introduction

Managers have two powerful ways of improving the performance and productivity of their subordinates, which are **counseling** and **on the job training**.

**Counseling** is the process of helping a subordinate define and resolve personal problems that affect performance or to develop a good attitude to work.

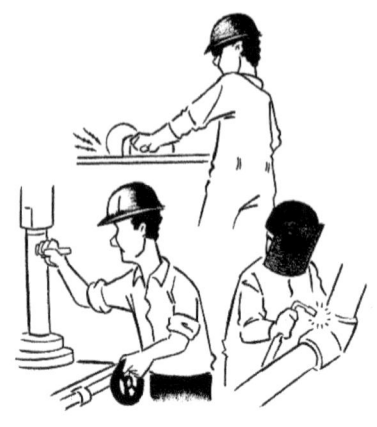
Someone will need help at some time

**On the job training** is the process of explaining, demonstrating and the structured supervision of specific skills or particular tasks. It is similar to the teaching process.

These are highly effective in three situations, which are:

## Resolving people problems

All managers are faced with problem people from time to time. Counseling and training are always the first considerations in these cases but they do not always result in success and sometimes more radical action is required. This is covered in the **Problem People** and **Positive Discipline** chapters.

## Maintaining group standards

The management of people both as individuals and groups is a dynamic process as nothing remains static – problems are always arising. A good manager must be aware of this and be constantly ready to use counseling and training to maintain standards.

## To achieve continuous improvement

The best way to avoid problems is to keep ahead of them by being proactive. You must have a plan for each individual in your group and for the group as a whole. In particular, new and inexperienced group members need special treatment so that they can meet required levels of performance.

Counseling and training share many of the same skills and in many cases they are used together to achieve your results. For example, you may have a young inexperienced person who is obviously having difficulty in performing a specific task, which you know he is capable of doing. This is an obvious example where training is needed but what is less evident is that a little bit of good counseling beforehand will enhance the training process. Perhaps the person is nervous or embarrassed about his lack of skills, which will need to be dealt with as the first priority.

Be alert to potential problems

We know from previous chapters that people are complex so don't expect them to always tell you about their problems or their needs. It is your responsibility as a manager to be constantly alert for the numerous warning signs.

The following are typical signs of change to look for then you must decide to initiate the counseling or training (or both) initiatives:

- Absenteeism
- Lack of interest
- Complaining
- Avoiding contact
- Depressed
- Argumentative
- Blaming others
- Laziness
- Irritable
- Lack of co-operation
- No initiative
- Does not communicate
- Making mistakes
- Poor quality
- Unsafe working
- Delegating to others
- Avoiding difficult work
- Lack of productivity

## *Counseling*

On-the-job counseling is a process of talking about things that affect the performance of the work. It involves sitting down in some quiet place and getting job problems out in the open without hurting each other. It's all about talking, listening, and trying to understand the other person's point of view. All supervisors are counselors whether they realize it or not. Sometimes a long heart-to-heart talk is needed to clear the air or a quick exchange will clear up a misunderstanding.

Counseling needs empathy

Perhaps the supervisor does most of the talking; the next time it may be the other way around. However, counseling is more than a casual discussion resulting from an accidental encounter. Counseling is a very effective management tool to increase productivity by solving problems and strengthening or repairing working relationships. Other kinds of problems of a very personal or psychological nature should be avoided and left to professionals in that field.

On-the-job counseling is normally initiated in one of two ways:

## 1. At the request of the worker

This is when the employee comes to the supervisor with a suggestion, problem, or complaint. Often these can be dealt with quickly without a structured counseling session but not always.

## 2. At the request of others

This happens when the actions or decisions of other departments or your bosses impact on one of your group. It is not unusual for the supervisor to end up with the need to counsel the worker.

## 3. By the supervisor

Most of the time, the supervisor initiates the process in a pro-active way. It is very important to identify the correct purpose for counselling, which must be based on improving the performance of the group. If you decide to counsel then you must have a good reason, firm objectives and be able to define the benefits to be gained. You cannot justify counseling as a way of changing aspects of other people simply because you do not like them.

Counseling is a sensitive process, which is why so many of us avoid it. It takes a good sense of timing, a smooth approach, and the personal confidence get things started. The most common problem is fear of the unknown, of getting involved in emotional human problems even if there are benefits to be gained. We will always find more important things to do; though it is difficult to imagine what can be more important than a problem affecting one of your groups. Overcome the fear and the process is simple and very rewarding.

Counseling is an essential skill when you are introducing significant change to the organization or to working methods.

| PRO-ACTIVE PURPOSES OF COUNSELLING | |
|---|---|
| • To resolve conflict within the group or between yourself and the group | • To discipline a group member |
| • To improve productivity | • To strengthen your relationships with individuals |
| | • To deal with the effects of change |

## *Preparation*

### Objectives

Make sure that you have your objectives clearly define and that you can justify them if necessary. These objectives must be consistent with company policy and other group objectives.

### Benefits

People will understand objectives better if they can identify them with real benefits. Try to associate objectives with measurable benefits.

### Choose the place and time

You will need to choose a place to hold the counseling session. Avoid noisy areas, uncomfortable places or the risk of continual interruptions. If your office is not suitable then borrow someone else's. Do not set up a counseling session too far in advance as it is human nature for the person involved to worry and possibly become emotional. Do it with minimum or zero lead in time.

## Choose the technique

Basically there are two distinct types of counseling techniques, which have almost opposite skill requirements. These are the *direct* and *indirect* techniques. It is very important to decide which technique you are going to use before you start the process. The directive technique is used when you do most of the talking and maintain fairly tight control of the discussion. The indirect technique is used when you do less talking and more listening to encourage the person to communicate more.

| THE DIRECTIVE TECHNIQUE IS BEST FOR: | THE INDIRECTIVE TECHNIQUE IS BEST FOR: |
|---|---|
| • A violation of company rules | • To change attitudes |
| • Unacceptable worker hostility | • Improve or repair relationships |
| • To correct mistakes | • To motive |
| | • To initiate or support change |

## *Choose the approach*

The most difficult part of the counseling process is getting started. Of course, the initial words will depend on the technique to be used and the seriousness of the reason for counseling. In time, you will work out your own starting words but, in the meantime, try starting as follows.

### Directive approach

*"Mike, we have to talk about your continual absenteeism and I hope that we can sort out a good solution."*

## Indirect approach

*"Mike, I have been concerned about the plant production levels and I thought it would be useful if we could discuss possible improvements."*

Get to the point quickly, state the facts and do not make personal accusations. Try to deal with the situation and try not to blame the person.

## Prepare a written agenda

Use your *everything book* to prepare a brief agenda for the meeting and use it.

# *The six steps*

## 1. The start

Try and start in a friendly way by asking how he is or something light to break the ice. Do not prolong this, as you need to move onto your prepared approach started and get to the subject matter without delay.

## 2. The purpose

Do not talk around the objectives for the meeting, even if the reasons are unpleasant.

## 3. Discuss performance

Talk about actual performance and how it has demonstrates the problem.

## 4. Identify improvement areas

Try to agree on improvement areas. Demonstrate how these relate to the aims of the group and the company.

## 5. Discuss possible solutions

You have many options including on the job training, using company documents, books, etc. The person may have their own solutions that they would like to discuss.

## 6. Agree an improvement plan

That's a great idea. I'll note it down

You must try and finalize on a positive note; there is nothing more positive than a set of defined and measurable objectives that both parties are committed to.

| TIPS FOR EFFECTIVE COUNSELLING | |
|---|---|
| • Speak in a quiet controlled voice | • Silence can help to give reflection time |
| • Avoid emotion | • Do not impose a time limit |
| • Do not argue | • Fully use your effective listening skills |
| • If the person is angry then let them talk until it subsides | • Show that you are interested |

## On the job training

Training is almost a natural human instinct. We all train our children without even thinking about it but when we have the job of training someone at work we find problems.

Our working environment is continually changing and our workforce need different skill sets to keep up. One solution is to replace existing people with new up to date workers. The problem with this is that the replacement of personnel is a very costly and risky exercise. In addition, your new worker will probably be out of date himself in a year or so and you are back with the same problem. On the job training is an obvious solution in most cases for the following reasons:

- It's very cost effective

- You don't lose an experienced worker

- You don't disrupt the group

- You avoid the learning curve of a new employee

- What happens if the new guy is not up to it?

However, there is one serious problem to consider which is that you must be realistic. In some cases there will be individuals that are simply not capable of reaching the new standards required.

On the job training is often a one to one situation, usually involving the supervisor and one of the group. The supervisor uses the actual work as the training location, and works with the trainee to improve skills or introduce new tasks.

On the job training can also involve one from the group who receives coaching from one of his colleagues. This is often called the buddy system where an inexperienced group member works along side a very competent member as a learning exercise. Another example is the employee receiving coaching from a manager from outside the group.

Nearly all the problems associated with on the job training are very simple to overcome. Like so many other parts of our work they require us to take a more systematic approach to the situation.

Most workers usually take pride in learning a new skill. These new skills are to our mutual benefit as it is good for the worker to improve employment value and for us to have new capability in our groups. In addition, by making learning possible, you earn their respect and build enduring relationships.

The supervisor is frequently the only person in the organization that teaches the basic knowledge and the many key skills that the group needs to learn. On-the-job training should never stop.

| SUPERVISORS MUST SHOW THEIR GROUP – HOW TO . . . | |
|---|---|
| • Operate machines | • Comply with company rules |
| • Complete forms | • Improve productivity |
| • Understand procedures | • Enhance safety |
| • Complete reports | • Use tools |
| • Perform tasks more effectively | • Maintain equipment |

## Don't be a schoolteacher

Adults do not learn in the same way as children do in school or at home. Do not talk down to adults or you will build barriers and probably be insulting.

| DON'T SAY . . . | SAY . . . |
|---|---|
| Let me teach you how to do this | Let's figure out how you can do this quickly, comfortably, and correctly |
| Let me teach you to do it right the first time | Let me show you how I do this, and you can figure out the best way for you to do it |

Another important mistake to avoid is simply telling someone what to do. People learn by doing and repeating what they have been shown. The reality is that adults learn differently to the process we all experienced as children. The main motivation for the adult learner is to see a benefit to gaining new knowledge and skills. Very few adults have the time or interest in listening to abstract theories and concepts.

## The three areas for on the job training

### 1. Induction or orientation

Induction is the process of giving basic information, instructions and general orientation to new members of your group. This is an essential responsibility, which helps new employees enormously and reduces the wastage of your time. The easiest way to cover inductions is to prepare basic induction notes, which can be used time and time again.

## 2. Opportunist

As a supervisor, you have daily opportunities to provide instruction. Every time you see someone that could do with help then you have identified another opportunity.

## 3. Planned training

Planned training can be a company initiative or the basic activity of being a supervisor. You should be continually monitoring both the performances of your group and the individuals involved. You should have a training plan for each individual and an objective for the group. We will cover this later in the book.

# *Get prepared*

### How much time can you allow?

How long can you allow the learner to reach this standard? It the job takes an hour and is done once per month you need to be able to teach it quickly or you will simply be employing two people's time instead of one. Be realistic but set a time so that both the learner and the trainer have a target to work to. It may pay to set times at which intermediate targets should be reached. In time you may build up a fairly accurate picture of the time someone who is going to be satisfactory takes to reach a certain point. This might help you decide whether it is worthwhile continuing the training of someone who is nowhere near this intermediate standard in the time.

### Analyze the job

Do the job slowly yourself, or get someone else to do it while you note down what happens. You will almost certainly miss something if you simply try to think through a job. Make sure you remember the starting point and the finish point. A learner forms good habits by having them as part of the learning drill - not as something learned later. Obviously you must set a very good example yourself on such things as cleaning up and setting out carefully so that waste is minimized.

## Get the facts

Decide what facts are required for the essential knowledge: such things as timings, dimensions, quantities, qualities, who to go to for authority, weight limits, reference materials, etc.

## What standard must be achieved?

How will you and the jobholder know when they are doing the job properly? This is a very important decision. The standard set must meet the MINIMUM required.

## Identify the skills

Look through the list of activities, which make up the job and decide which ones take skill.

## Tools and materials

What tools, materials, equipment, reference information or records are required before starting the job? You look foolish if you start to teach something and find that some material you need is out of stock.

If possible use the real tools and materials from the very beginning. Otherwise there is a possible problem of confidence to be faced later. Of course you would only do this after considering potential costs.

## Safety

Evaluate all possible dangers and health risks to self and others. Remember that something may not be a danger to you - because you are familiar with the equipment but it may be a danger to a learner.

Ooops!

## Short cuts

Are there any special tips, which you have learned on the basis of experience, and IS IT SAFE FOR THE LEARNER TO USE THEM? This is an important question and may lead you to abandon an unsafe method yourself. If it is not safe for the learner it is unlikely to be safe for anyone - they just have a better chance of getting away with it.

## The Four-Step Process

The following process of four steps has been successfully used for many years.

| | |
|---|---|
| **1 Prepare the worker** | Assess the level of knowledge and skill that the worker already has. Do not waste time (or insult the employee) by telling them something they already know. It may be that a short refresher session is all that is necessary. Explain clearly what you are going to teach and why. Try to create interest in the process by linking it with benefits |
| **2 Explanation and demonstration** | Firstly, you tell the person how to do it, and why it is done that way. You allow them to ask you questions. Then, you show the person how to do it, again inviting questions |
| **3 Supervised imitation** | You allow the learner to do it while you give guidance. No matter how good your explanation and demonstration the worker only really learns by doing it himself |
| **4 Follow up** | It is important to perform follow-up reviews to ensure that standards are being maintained |

# CHAPTER 15

# PROBLEM PEOPLE

| | |
|---|---:|
| • Introduction | 192 |
| • Recognize that a problem exists | 192 |
| • Reasons for problems | 193 |
| • Evidence of problems | 193 |
| • Basic management tools for resolving problems | 194 |
| • Reacting to the problem employee | 194 |
| • Key success factors | 195 |
| • What to do when all else fails | 196 |
| • Practical examples of coaching | 197 |
| • Practical examples of counseling | 198 |

## Introduction

As we have discussed earlier, management is all about getting things done through other people. It should be obvious that if the other people have problems and difficulties, then these may create barriers to getting things done. An important aspect of a manager's job is to Identify when subordinates have problems and be skilled at resolving them Don't forget that one person's problem can also effect the performance of the group as a whole, in terms of effectiveness, productivity, etc.

## Recognize that a problem exists

The first task for the manager is to recognize that a problem exists. You cannot always wait until the person involved asks for help as too much damage could occur. Many people find that admitting to problems is not easy, particularly to the boss, so you must take the initiative in such cases.

Wow, something's wrong!

Throughout this book we stress the importance of spending time with your group. Effective MBW (management by walkabout) will ensure that you are sensitive to changes in individual and group behavior. For example, you should be sensitive for behavior changes such as:

- Lack of communication
- Immature behavior
- Intentionally ignoring or avoiding you
- Excessive absenteeism
- Inexplicable lowering of work quality or production

## Reasons for problems

Usually, there are three reasons people don't get the job done. Regardless of what reason people may give, the answer may be one these three:

| REASONS FOR NOT GETTING IT DONE . . . . | |
|---|---|
| Lack of knowledge or skill | • No instruction, orientation or training given<br>• Poor or no feedback of work done |
| Restrictions | • A physical restriction.<br>• Lack of time.<br>• Materials or tool problems |
| They don't want to | • Has a gripe<br>• Stress<br>• Unhappy with supervisor or role<br>• Negative attitude |

## Evidence of problems

As a supervisor, you may have to rely on your own skill to recognize signs of performance or attitude problems. What are some of the signs of declining performance? What are some of the signs of a poor attitude?

| KEY POINTS | |
|---|---|
| Signs of declining performance include:<br>• Decreased productivity.<br>• Poor quality work.<br>• Missed due dates.<br>• Doing small tasks first.<br>• Avoiding tougher jobs.<br>• Disorganization.<br>• Relying on others for directions.<br>• Upward delegation.<br>• Absenteeism. | Signs of a poor attitude include:<br>• Little or no initiative.<br>• Withdrawn.<br>• Lack of interest.<br>• Increased complaining.<br>• Being uncooperative.<br>• Blaming failure on others.<br>• Acting defensive.<br>• Avoiding contact with others on team.<br>• Lacking enthusiasm for job.<br>• Irritability, depression. |

## Basic management tools for resolving problems

All managers can develop the 3 basic management tools for resolving problems. They do not always work but they have an impressive record.

| THREE MANAGEMENT TOOLS FOR RESOLVING PROBLEMS | |
|---|---|
| COUNSELING | Counseling is an active method where supervisor helps an employee define and resolve personal problems that affect the job performance. |
| ON THE JOB TRAINING | On the Job training is a process initiated by a supervisor to train an employee in the knowledge and skills required in the work place. |
| POSTIVE DISCIPLINE | Positive discipline is the process of establishing behavior standards that all employees have to maintain. |

Counseling, on the job training and positive discipline are closely related and often overlap. Each approach needs special attention but they also have many shared skills.

## Reacting to the problem employee

Up to now, we have discussed controlled situations where supervisors identify problems and initiate corrective action. In these cases the supervisor has time to think about and plan these actions. However, supervisors must occasionally deal with an employee who is being disruptive, hostile or even aggressive. It is clear that in these cases the supervisor has to defuse the immediate situation before being able to initiate the three management tools. This can be a key situation for the supervisor because if not handled well the situation can become emotionally charged and the only solution will be serious discipline and discharge. One moment of madness can easily ruin years of good service. It is your job to **control** these flash points by taking assertive action.

## *Key success factors*

- Do not avoid the problem. Time will not solve it

- Keep your own emotions under control. Let the other person release anger without an immediate reaction on your part. Often this simple act results in an apology and the problem being resolved

- Use your listening skills. Find out what the real problem is

Control your emotions!

- Consider the problem and not the person. Do not take things personally

- Try to defuse the problem in a calm manner, by suggesting, *let's have a private chat about this.* Start to use your counseling skills

- Show interest and take it seriously. Use the positive communication skills that you have learned

## What to do when all else fails

Sometimes, in spite of all your efforts, it is clear that these three management tools just are not going to work. The supervisor must take action in such cases, as inaction will almost always cause many more problems. There are usually three remaining options, which are:

| | |
|---|---|
| **1 Restructure existing job role** | This is a difficult option to take because it can often result in resentment or embarrassment. Nobody likes to see their job changed for apparent inability. Use this approach with great care, as it can easily become a management cop out (evasion) |
| **2 Transfer employee elsewhere** | This is a viable option if it is clear that another productive role exists. However, make sure that you are not taking this as a soft option and giving the problem to someone else to resolve |
| **3 Serious disciplinary action** | A good manager will never enjoy this task but it has to be done on occasions. This is discussed in more detail in the POSITIVE DISCIPLINE chapter |

## *Examples of situations that may require coaching*

- Orientation and training of a new employee
- Teaching a new job skill
- Need to explain standards of work
- Need to explain cultural norms and political realities of the organization
- Where simple corrections to performance are required
- Goals or business conditions change
- You are new to a group
- Employees facing new work experience
- Employee that needs help setting priorities
- Follow up to a training session
- Employee that displays low or moderate performance
- Employee who needs reinforcement for good performance
- Employee wants to become a peak performer
- Formal or informal performance reviews
- Employee needs preparation to meet future career goals
- Employee needs preparation for more challenging work assignment
- Employee needs to develop self-confidence
- When power or control battles are affecting team cohesiveness

Can you think of any other situations that may require coaching?

## *Examples of situations that may require counseling*

- Reorganizations
- Lay-offs - counseling for those who are laid off and those who are not
- Demotions due to organization changes
- Salary freezes; decreases in salary, status or responsibility
- Employee faced with other career opportunities inside or outside of the organization
- Employee faced with no career opportunities inside or outside of the organization
- Employee unhappy with you as a boss
- Employee problem with work assignment
- Employee who has conflict with a peer
- Employee that feels stressed or burned out
- Employee who feels insecure about skills or ability to do the job
- Employee quitting to take new job.
- Employee who has been promoted and is scared
- Employee's personal problems are affecting performance of others
- Performance problems that persist
- Employee who is experiencing failure
- Employee who is disappointed in a new job

Can you think of any other situations from your personal experience where counseling would have been effective?

# CHAPTER 16

# POSITIVE DISCIPLINE

| | | |
|---|---|---|
| • | Introduction | 200 |
| • | Discipline line | 200 |
| • | Consistency | 201 |
| • | Well communicated | 201 |
| • | Reasonable and justifiable | 202 |
| • | Flexibility | 202 |
| • | Immediacy | 203 |
| • | Privacy | 203 |
| • | The "Hot Stove Rule" | 204 |
| • | Minor misdemeanors | 205 |
| • | Serious disciplinary issues | 205 |
| • | Working within the system | 207 |

## Introduction

The word discipline has a negative sound, we immediately think of authority and punishment. However, there is another more constructive way to think about this which we can call – POSITIVE DISCIPLINE.

Positive discipline is all about creating an orderly environment where people can conduct themselves to agreed standards of behavior to the benefit of everyone. In this way we avoid unnecessary conflict and potential accidents. Most family groups establish an atmosphere of Positive Discipline, which protects individuals' rights but also develops harmony in the family. In addition, Positive Discipline is an excellent learning medium for our children, which protects their safety and development.

Avoid negative discipline

Discipline that is NEGATIVE tends to create conflict and damages group harmony. Negative discipline occurs when subordinates disobey the rules or reluctantly accept them.

## Discipline line

The first step is to establish and maintain a reasonable, but firm discipline line. This line is a well-defined, well-communicated set of behavior standards that you expect all employees to maintain. This will tell an employee what is expected and what is not permitted. It is essential to set a reasonable, justifiable and consistent discipline line. The key success factors are:

## Consistency

This means that at times when there is an infraction then the appropriate disciplinary action is taken irrespectively of who is involved! Of course, the action you take will vary according to the seriousness of the circumstances and the person involved. An innocent first offender may be treated in a different way to someone who repeatedly offends. The important thing is that you take action. A lack of consistency will create confusion among your group and inevitably reduce respect for you, the supervisor. Inconsistency is often associated with favoritism, which will damage your relationship with the group. There are many ways to reward people but allowing them to break the discipline rules in not one of them.

## Well communicated

Most companies have procedures or customs for informing personnel about company rules and standard of behavior. However, in many cases you will have specific rules within the group. For example, you may decide to limit certain activities due to the inexperience of your group. Another more mature group may not have these restrictions. Never assume that everyone knows these company or local rules. All new employees should be well inducted before joining the group. If you have any doubts about the rest of your group then get them together and hold a refresher meeting.

An interesting feature of rules in industry and in life in general is the numerous examples of de facto rules and customs. That is to say, rules that have simply been established with little or no justification. For example, the sign may say NO SMOKING but everyone ignores it and always has done so. In some cases these are best left alone if they do not represent a serious problem. However, if you do decide to enforce them then tell everyone first. DO NOT set an example by suddenly disciplining someone. All you will achieve will be a lack of respect and derision.

## *Reasonable and justifiable*

Rules need reasons and objectives and if these are missing then they will rightly receive little respect. Unreasonable rules are difficult to maintain and cause an unnecessary management burden. Why not check out new rules by passing them by the SMART Objective test first.

## *Flexibility*

Of course, some rules have to be rigid and inflexible particularly where safety or protecting the environment is involved. However, there is considerable room for flexibility where the discipline is set in other areas. For example, creative environments such as design or fashion agencies may have very low discipline lines. Be careful as there are advantages and disadvantages in both high and low discipline lines. Think about it and set yours to suit the requirements of the company and your group. If you change the level of the line then communicate and justify it before implementing it.

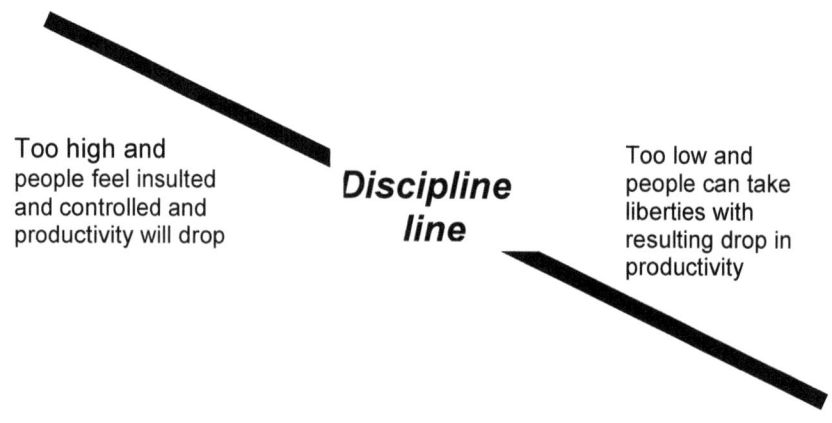

One good tip is to always err on the side of stronger leadership or in other words a higher discipline line. Most individuals and groups prefer firm leadership to weakness. It is always easier to raise the line later than to try to lower it.

## *Immediacy*

The discipline process must start as soon as possible after the infraction becomes known. Of course, you should not take action until you know the facts, and enough time must be allowed to dissipate any emotions that may have been generated. In the case of clear infractions where there is no doubt then use the puppy rule. Young puppies that are not yet house-trained are taken to the scene of the crime immediately to be disciplined. The longer you leave it then the less effective will the correction factor be. Of course, I am not suggesting that we treat adults like our pets but this particular principle is very valid.

## *Privacy*

The discipline of an individual should never be done in public or where others can hear it. The old fashion of disciplining a person in front of everyone in order to set an example or to demonstrate your authority has no place in modern management. Your motives in discipline must be corrective and designed to make improvements and not to humiliate anyone.

## The "Hot Stove Rule"

However well you handle discipline it remains an unpleasant task that often causes resentment. The challenge to the supervisor is to apply the necessary disciplinary action so that it minimizes damage to individuals and to the supervisor himself. A really effective way to incorporate all the rules that are described above is to adopt the *hot stove rule*. When you touch a hot stove, the reaction is immediate, with warning, consistent, and impersonal. For example:

1. The burn is **immediate**; there is no doubt about the cause and effect

2. There was **advance communication**, since everyone knows what happens if he touches a stove when the stove is red hot

3. The result is **consistent**; every time a person touches a hot stove, he is burned

4. The result is **impersonal** because whoever touches a hot stove is burned. The burn was caused by the act of touching the stove, not because of who the person is. Discipline should be directed against the act and not against the person

The comparison between the "hot stove rule" and disciplinary action is obvious.

## Minor misdemeanors

A really good way to establish a positive discipline for the first time is to have a good spring clean within your group. It is possible that bad habits have been established that need to be eliminated. For example, maybe your people are leaving the job site too early or taking too many coffee breaks. This needs to be dealt with firmly but diplomatically. After all it is as much your fault as theirs. Get them together and use your communication skills to explain what needs to change and why. This type of exercise is much more effective if other supervisors are involved with the support of your boss.

## Serious disciplinary issues

Unfortunately, there are times when all your best efforts fail or when someone commits an infraction that demands serious discipline, all of which could result in the dismissal of the offender. We can divide these into two categories, as follows:

### Serious breach of company rules

All companies will have disciplinary procedures to cover serious infractions. Examples are:

- Serious safety violations
- Theft of company property
- Continual absence from work
- Assault on company property or other employees
- Falsification of records or time cards
- Criminal behavior
- Gross insubordination

These types of infractions require formal action; they cannot be dealt with at supervisor and group level. It is the supervisor's responsibility to initiate the discipline process in all such cases. If there are extenuating circumstances then these will be dealt with as part of the formal process.

## Performance standards

Another important reason for serious discipline is where an individual performance constantly fails to meet your standards or those of the company. The decision to take this action will, in many cases, be based on the judgement of the supervisor. However, this final action must follow the failure of counseling or on the job training and the lack of another solution (transfer to another department etc.). This represents one of the most difficult aspects of a good supervisor's role. For example, it may involve the dismissal of a willing, enthusiastic nice person. It is important to be objective and impersonal in this area by concentrating on performance and capability and not the person.

You have to think it through!

Before taking action the supervisor should assure himself by asking:

1. Have I given the employee every chance to succeed? Would more counseling or training resolve the problem?
2. Have I clearly established what is required? Does the employee understand the expectations and job standards?
3. Has the employee made promises to improve and not kept those promises?

4. Is the individual's performance disrupting the team's performance or affecting business results?

5. Am I certain that I am not acting on personal preference? It is unjustifiable to discipline someone simply because you do not like him.

Remember that your responsibility as a supervisor is to protect your company's interests and maintain the harmony and effectiveness of your group. Confirmed under-performers will simply undermine all your other good work and they will continually waste your precious time. Another important factor is that this type of discipline usually benefits the individual too in the longer term. He will now be released to seek a future more suited to his skills. SO DON'T BE SOFTY IN THIS IMPORTANT AREA.

## *Working within the system*

It is fundamental that the supervisor ensures that he is working within the organization's policies and procedures when initiating the disciplinary process. Many companies have well defined procedures that have been developed that comply with the law, trade union agreements and general business objectives. It is your responsibility to know these procedures and use them in all cases. If you have any doubts about these then consult your superiors. The typical steps in the disciplinary process are:

1. Verbal warnings

2. Written confirmations

3. Termination discussion

However, it is probable that your company has developed these further. For example, it is possible that the individual's trade union representative must attend any meeting held or receive copies of letters. Failure to observe these rules can result in the disciplinary action being cancelled or damaging legal action. In either case, you will end up with more problems than you started with and **you** are now guilty of an infraction. Always work within the system.

## Involve your boss

It is important the supervisor ensures that his own superior will support his decisions. It is sensible to keep him fully informed and ready to approval and support your actions. You may find that your superior can positively assist you by suggesting other alternatives.

What do you think?

## Records

The supervisor needs to keep an informal file of each employee which records dates and times of the warnings issued, counseling and training sessions. Don't forget that you may be called on to justify your actions to your superior or in a court of law.

# CHAPTER 17

# PEOPLE PLANNING

| | | |
|---|---|---|
| • | Introduction | 210 |
| • | Get yourself informed | 212 |
| • | Typical development plan for people | 214 |
| • | Determine the correct management style to use | 215 |
| • | Style selection chart | 218 |
| • | People planning approach | 219 |
| • | Increase productivity through motivation | 221 |
| • | Building and maintaining relationships | 224 |
| • | Relationship channels | 224 |
| • | Tips on building good relationships | 225 |
| • | Your behavior | 227 |
| • | The super Z manager specification | 228 |

## *Introduction*

ALL the evidence from modern theorists, the Japanese success story and from the top international companies is that corporate success depends on the **Leadership** and **Motivation** of people. However, it is amazing that so many companies and managers fail to grasp this opportunity by not putting it into ACTION.

How many times do we hear from companies that *our people are our most important resource*? You will see this type of statement in company brochures, annual accounts, statements to shareholders etc. There is no doubt that these are all based on good faith but to what extend does this policy filters through the organization? NOT MUCH!

Most managers seem to be pre-occupied with machines and the technical aspects of their work. This is in spite of a mountain of evidence that proves that the key to future success is our ability to manage people effectively at all levels in the organization. The problem is that managing technology and machines can be easily defined and understood whereas people management tends to be abstract and difficult to deal with.

Let's see if we can simplify the problems and develop a practical model that will be effective in the real world. Maybe, a good way to approach **people management** is to adopt the basic approach we take with **machines**. For example, machines have technical files (procedures, specifications, performance standards etc.), planned maintenance systems, corrective action procedures and many other supporting methods. Why not treat people, at least, in the same way and with the same importance. In addition, this would be totally consistent with our toolbox style approach that we discussed earlier. Let's look at the key points that we can easily do.

| 1. Get yourself informed | Time required | Cost |
|---|---|---|
| Getting to KNOW your group and the individuals is the first key step. You need to determine all the strengths, weaknesses and potential before you can start to think about making improvements. | 5 hours max. | NIL |

| 2. Determine the style to use | Time required | Cost |
|---|---|---|
| The Leadership chapter demonstrated that we need to determine the maturity of our group and to adopt the matching style. This is step two | 2 hours max. | NIL |

| 3. People planning | Time required | Cost |
|---|---|---|
| We do it for machines so why not or people | 8 hours | NIL |

| 4. Motivate productivity through motivation | Time required | Cost |
|---|---|---|
| We now need to build and maintain relationships and define the motivating factors that we learned before into a simplified practical form that can easily become part of our routine behavior. This is our PREVENTIVE MAINTENANCE program for people | 30 seconds | NIL |

In this chapter we will learn how to improve productivity dramatically for a mere investment of a few hours and at negligible cost. Let's look at these steps in more detail.

## *Get yourself informed*

You would never attempt to resolve the problems of a machine or undertake a major maintenance or modification without knowing how the machine functions and its operating characteristics. On the other hand we are very complacent about our people, we assume that they are what they are and normally accept the situation. The truth is that few of us realize the untapped potential for productivity that exists.

The human machine works!

Our first step in treating people as equal to machines is to analyze each person to identify current problems, create a betterment plan and introduce the appropriate planned maintenance program.

## Basic analysis

It is relatively easy to analyze everyone in your group; it takes a little time, an organized approach and some lateral thinking. The enclosed example form may help in designing your own specific document. Once the format has been prepared then it is relatively easy to fill in and re-evaluated every month. Your first attempt may include many instinctive judgements but these will become more objective as you continue the exercise over the months. You should be able to complete each analysis in around 30 minutes by concentrating on key points and not getting bogged down in detail. So if you have ten people in your group then your initial time investment is around 5 hours. Sorting out just one troublesome machine can take that long!

Of course, you may get a surprise and find that you don't have enough information about the person to accurately complete the form. This is a clear warning sign that you have not been giving enough attention to your most critical resource - your people. In this case you must take immediate action by diplomatically checking with others, looking at records and by talking to the person. You will not get all the information the first time around but you will soon start to build a picture in your mind.

## Objectives and priorities

The next step is to evaluate your analysis and determine the objectives, priorities and summary actions required. These are the first steps in the planning process. Use the SMART objective test and the PARETO method to help you in this task.

## Documentation

Don't do this exercise on scraps of paper or in your normal work books. This subject demands its own dedicated and structured documentation, which must be treated as **highly confidential**. Think about doing it at home.

The following chart shows how easy it is to prepare a person evaluation. You can easily prepare a basic form that suits your own requirements in an hour or so, which can be photocopied and re-used time and time again.

Keep a permanent record of your most important resources – your people!

## *Typical development plan for people*

| PERSONAL AND CONFIDENTIAL | | | | |
|---|---|---|---|---|
| PERSONAL DEVELOPMENT PLAN FOR: John Doe (Tech. Gr. 1) | | | | DATE: 12/06/2012 |
| Legend: 1 = Nil  2 = Poor  3 = Basic  4 = Competent  5 = Specialist | | | | SUPERVISOR W Andrews |
| ANALYSIS | Cent. Pumps | Air Compressors | Gas Turbines | Relief Valves |
| **1. KNOWLEDGE LEVEL** | | | | |
| Existing | 3 | 3 | 4 | 1 |
| Planned | 4 | 4 | 4 | 1 |
| Action required | Yes | Yes | No | No |
| Priority | 2 | 1 | | |
| **2.  SKILL LEVEL** | | | | |
| Existing | 3 | 3 | 4 | 1 |
| Planned | 4 | 4 | 4 | 1 |
| Action required | Yes | Yes | No | No |
| Priority | 2 | 1 | | |

| 3.  ATTITUDE | Level | Comments |
|---|---|---|
| Enthusiastic? | 3 | This will improve when I have introduced the key success factors |
| Good group member? | 3 | This will improve when I have introduced the key success factors |
| Works within the rules? | 2 | Takes shortcuts and ignores procedures. I need to talk to him about this |
| Accepts instructions? | 3 | No problems here |
| Good timekeeper? | 4 | OK, this was a problem but I have resolved it. I need to keep a check on this though |
| Absenteeism? | 4 | No problems here |
| Keen to learn? | 5 | Will enjoy training |
| Does he have problems? | ? | I am not sure but his overall attitude seems to have changed. He is very reticent now |
| Potential supervisor? | YES | I need to keep an eye on this. He may need another year to be ready |

4 = Excellent     3 = Acceptable     2 = Poor     1 = Problem

**4. ACTION PLAN**

1. Check out best method of improving Air compressor knowledge and skills
2. Perform a low key counseling session to see if he has problems
3. Explain to him that his shortcuts are not acceptable

## *Determine the correct management style to use*

As we discussed in the leadership chapter, we have to consider the needs of the group as well as the individuals. A group is much more than the simple sum of the individuals. In time, groups form strong internal relationships, which can develop into positive and negative consequences for the supervisor. Although individuals are very important you must also consider the needs of the group. Research has shown that as few as 10% of the people tended to defy the group by producing outside the group norm. In consequence, performance improvements must be aimed at the group as well as individuals.

As we discussed earlier our management style needs to be adjusted to suit the maturity of the group. The following chart defines the elements of group maturity.

| GROUP MATURITY IS ALL ABOUT LEVELS OF - | |
|---|---|
| **Knowledge** <br> = <br> • Understands groups objectives <br> • Knows company procedures <br> • Is technically competent <br> • Knows the tasks to be done | **Skills** <br> = <br> • Can use tools competently <br> • Can consistently perform tasks <br> • Can work safely <br> • Maintains work quality standards |
| **Motivation** <br> = <br> • Is enthusiastic <br> • Communicates well <br> • Productive | **Self Sufficiency** <br> = <br> • Sorts out their own problems <br> • They help each other <br> • Need little outside discipline <br> • Accepts responsibility <br> • Confident |

The next step is to match maturity with styles using a simplified classification of four styles.

| STYLE | GROUP BEHAVIOR | MANAGER'S PEOPLE SKILLS |
|---|---|---|
| **1** <br> **DIRECTIVE** <br> High emphasis on tasks less on relationships | New group needs outside leadership <br> Unable to solve problems <br> Unsure on how to approach work | Discipline <br> Being able to perform tasks <br> Must be visible and available |
| **2** <br> **ENCOURAGING** <br> Tasks and relationships have equal importance | Still being developed as a team <br> Unable to solve problems <br> Capable of doing routine tasks | Problem solving <br> Task knowledge <br> Briefing and informing <br> Must be available |
| **3** <br> **SUPPORTIVE** <br> High emphasis on relationships less on tasks | Group is not fully developed as a team <br> Able to solve quite complex problems <br> Fully capable of doing tasks | On the job training <br> Delegation <br> Getting feed-back <br> Listening |
| **4** <br> **TRUSTING** <br> Stand back and let them get on with it | Group is an integrated team <br> Fully capable of performing all tasks <br> Group and manager have common objectives | Counseling <br> Inter-personnel |

Charts like the one above are interesting and are good for focusing attention, but they should not be taken too literally. You must look at your own group and decide which style is required. Never forget that as your group matures you need to adjust your style. Do not be surprised if your group behavior deteriorates following individual changes or as complacency sets in.

This is all very similar to the work of a school football coach who needs to teach individuals basic skills and behavior standards but he also has to develop the team as a whole (the group). Both these activities will be consistent with each other, as he knows that as individuals improve then the group will benefit.

The following chart can help you with the thought process.

### STYLE SELECTION CHART

| COMPETENCE | | ATTITUDE | | MATURITY LEVEL | TYPE OF STYLE |
|---|---|---|---|---|---|
| Knowledge | Skills | Motivation | Self-sufficiency | | |
| HIGH | H | H | H | HIGHEST | 4 |
| HIGH | H | H | L |  | 4/3 |
| HIGH | H | L | H |  | 3/4 |
| HIGH | H | L | L |  | 3 |
| HIGH | L | A | H |  | 2/3 |
| HIGH | L | A | L |  | 2 |
| HIGH | L | L | H |  | 2/1 |
| HIGH | L | L | L | MEDIUM | 2/1 |
| LOW | H | H | H |  | 2 |
| LOW | H | H | L |  | 2 |
| LOW | H | L | H |  | 2 |
| LOW | H | L | L |  | ½ |
| LOW | L | H | H |  | 1 |
| LOW | L | H | L |  | 1 |
| LOW | L | L | H |  | 2/1 |
| LOW | L | L | L | LOWEST | 2 |

## *People planning approach*

Machines perform best when they are included into good planned maintenance systems. This requires that each maintainable item and sometimes their associated systems have specific strategies allocated. These will include time based preventive maintenance, condition monitoring and advanced analytic methods such as RCM. All these individual strategies are then consolidated into the plant maintenance system, which is consistent with the company business objectives. It is a very wise policy to get each maintainable item into an acceptable condition before fully implementing the system. It is very difficult to perform planned maintenance on a machine that is continually breaking down!

Our next step is to prepare our people plan. It is no different to our other plans. It has activities, durations, start and finish dates etc. We will use all the skills that we learned in the earlier sections.

There are six steps in this process, which are detailed on the following chart:

| THE BASIC PLANNING STEPS | ACTIONS |
|---|---|
| 1<br><br>OBJECTIVES AND PRIORITIES | You already have these established during the analysis stage. However, these may need to be revised because there may be some conflict between the needs of the individual and the group. For example, you may decide that the whole group is weak on pumps and that becomes priority 1 for everyone. This allows you to set up one training plan instead of numerous individual ones. Don't forget that group priorities are often more important than individuals ones |
| 2<br><br>SCOPE OF WORKS | This is your action list that meets the requirements of your objectives |
| 3<br><br>DETERMINE METHODS | You have 3 methods available to you:<br><br>1. Training<br>2. Counseling<br>3. Discipline<br><br>However, each of these management tools has alternative methods and rules. Each of these is covered in previous chapters |
| 4<br><br>ESTIMATE TIMES AND RESOURCES | Both time and resources are finite. Don't be too ambitious. It is better to do a few things well than fail with them all. If you worried about this then re-look at your priorities and re-arrange them to reduce your workload. |
| 5<br><br>PREPARE THE MAIN PLAN | Prepare a simple bar chart showing activities by group and by individuals. Indicate the start and end dates for each activity. See the typical example |
| 6<br><br>AGREE THE PLAN | Discuss the plan and its objectives with the individuals involved. Concentrate on technical performance only. Personal items must be directly attended to in the counseling or discipline processes. |

## *Increase productivity through motivation*

We now need to develop our people *preventative maintenance system* by establishing a high moral, using the motivating factors and building good relationships within the group. Let's look at each of these and see how we can develop practical working solutions.

### Moral

We must differentiate between moral and motivation, which are interrelated but not the same. Poor moral is usually caused by a lack of attention to the hygiene factors that we discussed earlier in the book. All modern theorists agree that these factors do not motivate but they will **de-motivate** and *moral* dives.

In an earlier chapter we developed the concept and use of the management functions. To get moral under control and optimize your ability to build relationships and to motive people you need to use these functions yet again. Use your planning, organizational and control skills to create and maintain the best working environment for relationships and motivation For example:

- **Establish group facilities**

In the section on organization we discussed these facilities. Motivation will come to abrupt stop if you cannot provide the information, equipment and facilities. In fact you have created an anti motivator when you next try to motivate.

- **Sort out major problems**

If there are known personal problems, or you discover some as part of your people planning exercise, then these should be attended to and resolved as fast as possible.

None of this means that you cannot proceed to the next step of building relationships and motivating but you must realize that poor moral will restrict your progress. Unfortunately, we cannot always resolve these problems because we rely on others in the organization that may not agree that a valid problem exists. In these cases, we have to work around the problem the best we can but at least we have shown interest and have supported our people.

## Motivating for production

In chapter 11 on Leadership we discussed many factors for motivating people. Let's see if we can summarize these as a basis for the PM program. Here are these same factors in a simplified practical form:

| **PEOPLE ARE MOTIVATED AND MADE HAPPY BY -** | |
|---|---|
| Seeing the leader | Research showed that **visible** management was the most effective motivator. Confidence in management was related to how often employees saw the managers rather than the quality of the decisions managers made |
| Being informed | People can only take interest in the Department and the Organization if they are given plenty of information about what is going on. This should not be limited to what they need to know but should include what they want to know |
| Being involved | People perform better if they feel that they are involved. This does not mean letting them make all the decisions but it does mean asking their opinions and discussing things. Who knows, you might learn something! |
| Having objectives | Objectives give meaning to work. We all work better if we know WHY we are doing What we are doing and WHY it is needed by a certain time.<br><br>People work well towards clear targets. Partly this is a game but more importantly it is an opportunity for them to feel proud of themselves and thereby raise their self-esteem |
| Feeling important | People need to feel important and that work has value. Even boring repetitive work is easier to do if it is seen as being valuable. The person must be treated as more important than his level of productivity. Look after the person and the productivity will look after itself. Positive actions such as counseling and training |

This is easily achieved by scheduling an informal discussion with each of your group individuals each week. This is not about resolving specific problems, this is about communication. For example:

1. Hello George, how's it going?

2. Did I tell you about the new pumps that we have ordered? Do you think that they will improve things?

Communications, communications and communications!

3. How are you getting on with the new objectives we discussed last week?

4. You certainly did a good job on the shutdown last week

Four simple questions and a few minutes of effective listening and positive communication and you have covered the 5 key success factors. Maybe 5 to 10 minutes and your weekly PM task is completed. It is all so easy to control. Make a list of each person on a chart or in your Everything Book and tick them off after each chat. 10 individuals could take you just over an hour a week, which is nothing for your most important resource.

The important point here is the **WILL** to do it and this means that you must organize your workload to provide the time to be able to do it.

## Building and maintaining relationships

The building, protecting and repairing of relationships is at the center of all our lives. Family life is the best possible example of relationships at work. You spend almost as much time in work as you do with your family so it is not surprising that relationships are considered of fundamental importance. The art of motivation is nothing new to us as we do it as a matter of routine in our lives. We motivate our children to succeed and we encourage our friends in their pursuits.

Building and maintaining relationships takes time and effort but these can be so easily lost. An excellent relationship developed over five years can be lost in a second due to a hasty comment or a sudden action. As a supervisor you will build and maintain thousands of relationships during your career so it is worth developing your relationship skills.

Although relationships and motivation are not exactly the same, they are totally inter-related. For example, when you successfully motivate someone to do something then that will improve your relationship. On the other hand, if you have a good relationship it becomes easier to motivate because you are trusted.

## Relationship channels

A good way of looking at the relationship between the supervisor and his group of people is to look at a series of psychological communication channels, which allow interaction. These channels not only provide direct communication links with each individual but they also communicate with the group as a whole. Like all flow channels they must be clean, without blockages, kept cool and well lubricated.

Experts tell us that the supervisor has 75 percent of the responsibility for the relationships with his group. In consequence, you have the main responsibility for the effectiveness of these channels. This challenge starts with your behavior because it is certain you get back the kind of behavior you send out. So it is important to read this section along with the sections on positive behavior and effective communications.

| | DON'T FORGET - |
|---|---|
| The elasticity factor | There is an elasticity factor to all relationships. Fortunately for the supervisor, most relationships will stretch before they break and this can provide both parties the opportunity of a second chance. This means that even the more serious breaks in a relationship line can be repaired. However, this should be considered as a last resort and the stretch should never be used intentionally. The risk is that a relationship can break at any moment. Even if you manage to repair relationships you cannot wipe out the negative memories which may take years to disappear. |
| All relationships are different | There are around 6 billion people in the world and there are not two people exactly the same. It follows that no two relationships will be exactly the same and each person must be treated differently. |

## *Tips on building good relationships*

### Build new relationships quickly and carefully

The advantage of new relationships is that they start from a clean slate. This is a great opportunity to build a healthy and lasting relationship. Be careful not to show favoritism, as you cannot damage the existing relationships in the process. If you are the new boy then you will need to work very hard to establish your relationships with your new group. You will be the center of attention so be careful.

## Relationships require constant attention

Do not take relationships for granted, as they need maintenance in the same way as complex machinery does. A common problem is to only talk to your people when there is a problem or a specific reason. This is a clear sign to everyone that the job is more important than the person is.

## Repair damage quickly

No matter how skillful you become in building relationships the occasional breaks are inevitable. When these happens you must act quickly, don't allow them to fester. It may be a simple misunderstanding that can be resolved in seconds or perhaps an apology is required.

## Don't build one relationship at the expense of another

It is possible that one member of your group needs much more attention than another. In building one relationship, it is easy to neglect the others. Make time for each group member and never allow your personal favoritism to show.

## Don't play games with relationships

A relationship is not a toy or an experiment that the supervisor is free to experiment with freely. A relationship is based on trust and this must be treated with respect.

## Keep the channel cool

The relationship line can become emotionally charged. Extreme emotional feelings can make the channel very hot. An emotional outburst is one of the easiest ways of damaging relationships.

## Separate business from pleasure

The best policy is not to mix business and pleasure. It is difficult to discipline someone if you are close friends. Of course, in many cases you will have been co-worker and friends with most of your group for many years and there is no justification for changing these relationships. However, you need to exercise caution in these relationships. Try to do business thing in work and social things outside – don't mix the two.

## React to relationship breakdown

Sometimes in spite of all your hard work you fail to build a workable relationship with someone under your supervision. It is difficult to admit defeat but it is also important to protect the other relationships in the group. This nearly always means removing the person from the group. This can be achieved by transferring the person or by his termination. Making these decisions is never a pleasant task, but in some cases it is inevitable. Ironically, this action is usually the best for both parties.

# *Your behavior*

The last but not the least important aspect of people management is your behavior. This is the one area where you have enormous advantages over machine management, which is that you have the choice. Others usually choose their machines and they can do little to change that, but the way you behave is **your choice**. Let's look at how a good manager needs to behave.

| THE SUPER Z MANAGER SPECIFICATION | |
|---|---|
| **MANAGER X-Y-Z** | He is a Z manager that wishes to be a Y manager and treats his people with respect. A Z manager always looks for ways to improve himself and others. |
| **I AM OK YOU ARE OK** | Takes a positive attitude to himself and others |
| **AGGRESSIVE-PASSIVE-ASSERTIVE** | Can be assertive, aggressive and passive as required but never to excessive levels. |
| **POSITIVE DISCIPLINE** | Sets and maintains a fair and open discipline line. Never have favorites. |
| **FLEXIBLE** | Adjusts his behavior to suit the needs of individuals and the group |
| **RELIABLE** | Honest and trustworthy. Always tries to keep his promises. Loyal to his people. |

Why not develop this chart further and add your own specifications.

# CHAPTER 18

# ACTION FOR SUCCESS

| | |
|---|---:|
| • Introduction | 230 |
| • Management by objectives | 231 |
| • The inevitability of change | 233 |
| • Overcoming the fear of change | 234 |
| • Reducing resistance | 234 |
| • Our first SMART objectives | 236 |
| • Prepare a simple plan | 239 |
| • Survival tips | 241 |

## Introduction

We have covered a multitude of concepts, theories and recommendations in the past chapters. Let's further develop the job description for a perfect supervisor (or manager).

| | SUPER Z SUPERVISOR<br>JOB DESCRIPTION |
|---|---|
| PERSONAL | • Must be Honest<br>• Must have integrity<br>• Must be intelligent<br>• Will be a caring person<br>• Be loyal to the company, the boss and the group<br>• Can work well under pressure<br>• Always smartly dressed |
| TIME MANAGEMENT | • Is able to plan to spend at least 40% of time supervising |
| BEHAVIOR SKILLS | • Can maintain positive focused attitude<br>• Can be assertive, aggressive and passive as required<br>• Can adjust style to match maturity |
| KNOWLEDGE | • Must have technical knowledge of work being performed<br>• Must know all relevant company policies and objectives<br>• Must fully understand the role and responsibilities of a supervisor<br>• Has a developed list of priorities |
| TECHNICAL SKILLS | • Uses MBO and Is a good planner, organizer and controller<br>• Is a good manager of time and workload<br>• Has ability to make decisions<br>• Can personally perform the work assigned to the group<br>• Is a competent trainer |
| INTER PERSONAL SKILLS | • Understand the skills required for good communication<br>• Understands the skills of leadership<br>• Communicates routinely<br>• Maintains a fair and consistent level of discipline<br>• Can provide quality information to the group<br>• Can give clear and understandable instructions<br>• Is a good listener<br>• Can create good relationships<br>• Can motivate the group<br>• Can effectively counsel the individuals in the group<br>• Can perform on the job training<br>• Can assist with problems caused by change |

That is quite a job specification. If you can honestly claim to be 100% proficient in every category then you would be eligible to be a senior management consultant!! In reality *nobody* can be perfect in every requirement at all times. We have to set ourselves reasonable **SMART OBJECTIVES**.

## Management by objectives

It is possible that you have discovered areas where you could improve your performance as a supervisor. However, you may be thinking that it will be impossible to learn everything suggested in this book and to make so many changes and to continue working in your existing position effectively. It is logical to think that if you have not got the time available now, then how can you find time for all this new stuff? Do not worry too much about this, as there are ways to achieve the impossible.

Do not try to achieve everything today or tomorrow. It may take a year or so to make the important changes and the rest may need a lot longer. It does not matter because it is much more effective to achieve little by little correctly than to fail in too much.

For example, consider the following statements:

| WHAT WE CAN TRY TO DO | THE REALITY |
|---|---|
| WE CAN DO SOME THINGS AT ALL TIMES | **OUR FIRST SMART OBJECTIVES**<br><br>We can choose an achievable level of change by selecting the most important and the *easy to do* recommendations. |
| WE CAN DO SOME THINGS SOME OF THE TIMES | **MEDIUM TERM OBJECTIVES**<br><br>This second level will happen naturally, as our FIRST SMART OBJECTIVES become our natural way of doing things. |
| WE CAN DO ALL THINGS SOME OF THE TIMES | **LONG TERM OBJECTIVES**<br><br>As we become more confident then we can add new objectives to our development plan. |
| WE CAN DO ALL THINGS AT ALL TIMES | THIS IS **NOT** AN OBJECTIVE- JUST A DREAM |

In this chapter we will discuss how to select our first SMART objectives and the following steps towards our long-term objectives. However, before moving on to this, we have to consider a major barrier to our progress, which is the FEAR OF CHANGE. Everything that we do to improve our management skills will involve change for yourself, your subordinates and all around you. Unless you understand the effects of change you will never fully realize your objectives. So your first objective must be to use skills that we have already discussed in order to create the environment for the objectives to succeed.

## The inevitability of change

> Somebody said:
>
> "Why do you resist change? Do you wish to be dead? Only those things that are dead do not change."

Change is inevitable and it will happen with your help or without it. You may be a traditional person who likes life as it is. But your life has changed all around you since your childhood and it will continue to do so for you, your children and theirs. Of course, you don't have to like it and you can even resist it but you will not stop it. To be an effective manager you must try to understand change and use the benefits to your and the company's benefit.

You have a greater problem than most other people do because you have to overcome your own natural resistance to change and convince the people that work for you too.

## Overcoming the fear of change

The biggest problem with effecting change is the fear that it creates such as: Feeling too old to learn new techniques or technology; Changes in relationships in the working team; Fear of being embarrassed in front of others; Fear of losing promotion opportunities or even their own job. The following chart identifies change factors:

| FACTORS WHICH AFFECT ATTITUDE TO CHANGE ||
|---|---|
| Habit | If someone has grown up and lived with a lot of change they accept change as normal. There will be more resistance from someone who has done the same job and lived in the same place for a long time. |
| Social and cultural beliefs | These will be related to a particular community, class, trade or even work-group where historically they have been the victims of change rather than the beneficiaries. |
| Personal sense of security | Worries about security caused by mortgage, marriage, divorce, debts, all make people more liable to resist change because any new situation feels less secure than the known situation. |
| Loyalty and trust | Resulting from past relationships and experiences with you, management generally, and working groups. |
| Historic events | The ways in which past changes have affected them personally. |
| Specific apprehensions | Fear that their trade or industry is dying. |
| The way in which the change is introduced | Consultation, timing, delay before any benefit is seen etc. |

## *Reducing resistance*

Change management is a relatively new management concept and it is a complex subject that is beyond the scope of these chapters. Most of your changes will affect you directly but many will have indirect effects on your group. Let's look at two ways that you can adopt to reduce the negative effects of change.

## Be strong and confident

This easy to say, isn't it? Many of the new things that we are going to adopt will feel strange and you may be embarrassed or nervous to try them for the first time. Remember the first time you dived into a swimming pool? Just do it. The next time will be easier.

## Empathize

Do you remember this word from a previous chapter? It means putting yourself in the other person's situation and trying to anticipate his concerns. Then you act to inform him or reassure him or whatever is necessary.

Major change needs far more consideration and actions.

| MAJOR CHANGES | |
|---|---|
| TAKE THE HARD DECISIONS QUICKLY | If change means that people need to be moved or even dismissed then do it as quickly and humanely as you can |
| REASSURE THE REST | Once the hard decisions have been made then reassure the rest that they are an important part of the future. Remove the fear |
| INFORM | Keep people informed about what is going on. You may not be able to tell them everything but tell them what you can. If you don't inform them then the *grapevine* will |
| INVOLVE | If people feel that they have an involvement in the planned change (part ownership) then they will usually respond positively. If it has been imposed on them then they will have less commitment to making it work |
| SELL BENEFITS | If participants see the benefits of change as a way of reducing their problems and not increasing them then you will be supported. |

A change strategy is very likely to fail if management:

- Fail to consider people and the threat to their roles and positions
- Fail to consider the difficulty people have in changing their ways
- Fail to provide effective training so that the new skills can be learned and accepted
- Fail to define the results expected
- Fail to monitor the change and provide guidance as needed

## *Our first smart objectives*

Our first step is to select our priorities and then to define our FIRST SMART OBJECTIVES. It is essential that these are realistic and achievable and that you do not try to overachieve. Let's look at our categories again.

- **We can do some things at all times**

Our first step is to choose those key success factors that will have the most impact on our performance. I have selected just four key activities for the initial objectives in the following order of priority.

1. KNOW YOUR ROLE

2. PREPARE PEOPLE PLANS

3. MANAGEMENT BY WALK AROUND

4. USE THE MOTIVATORS

These four key objectives are all covered in the chapters of this book and they are all SMART in terms of specific, achievable and realistic. In order to develop these into SMART objectives we now have to make them **measurable** and **time** bound. Let's check them out.

| KEY OBJECTIVES | S | M | A | R | T |
|---|---|---|---|---|---|
| KNOW YOUR ROLE | ✓ | Prepare a job specification | ✓ | ✓ | Set a time and duration |
| PREPARE PEOPLE PLANS | ✓ | Prepare a formal plan | ✓ | ✓ | Set a time and duration |
| MANAGEMENT BY WALK AROUND | ✓ | Keep a daily or weekly record | ✓ | ✓ | Set targets for each week over a reasonable period |
| USE THE MOTIVATORS | ✓ | Use your everything book to record contacts | ✓ | ✓ | Set yourself a time limit to consciously do it. |

The key objectives will also provide you with the basic foundation for achieving all your future objectives. Let's look at these in more detail.

## Know your role

This is the fundamental first step irrespective of how well your day is organized. If your current schedule does not allow you to directly supervise your group then you analyze the problem. It is important to obtain the support of your boss in this exercise otherwise you will always have an uphill struggle. Have a good look at the following:

- How much time do I spend on direct supervision?
- How much time is being spent on materials?
- How much time is being wasted on administration?
- How much time is being wasted on customs or activities that you cannot justify?
- Do you think that your company could improve your role in some way?

This step does not need a lot of time but it does need a period of very honest thinking and objective analysis. Allow at least a week to achieve all this.

## Prepare people plans

This takes a lot of thought but not a lot of time. Use the People Planning chapter as your guide. You should get it done in a week with maybe some work at home.

## Management by walk around

Once you have your role established then you have to effect the changes that allow you to spend more time with your people. This activity is the most difficult because you have to create the necessary time without disrupting your normal responsibilities. It is a bit of a chicken and egg situation. Check the chapters on time management and organization.

This is the key objective to your success. You must create time for MBWA by getting yourself organized. Once done then you need to use the communications and people skills to make the MBWA effective.

## Use the motivators

This takes WILL and CONFIDENCE. The more you do it, the easier it becomes.

## Prepare a simple plan

Now we can produce a simple plan based on a reasonable time period. I have chosen 12 weeks but you can make your own decision on how long you need. You need to think about each activity and evaluate the work involved and how you can integrate the additional work into your existing routines.

| KEY OBJECTIVES | WEEKS | | | | | |
|---|---|---|---|---|---|---|
| | 1 | 2 | 3 | 4 | 5 | 6 - 12 |
| 1. KNOW YOUR ROLE | ▬ | | | | | |
| 2. PREPARE PEOPLE PLANS | | ▬ | | | | |
| 3. MANAGEMENT BY WALK AROUND | | | ▬▬▬▬▬▬▬▬▬▬▬▬▬▬▬ | | | |
| 4. USE THE MOTIVATORS | | | | ▬▬▬▬▬▬▬▬▬▬▬▬ | | |

Always start a new activity on a separate week so that you can focus fully on the task. Set weekly or monthly targets for the longer activities. For example:

| TARGETS | MONTHS | | |
|---|---|---|---|
| | 1 | 2 | 3 |
| MANAGEMENT BY WALK AROUND | 2 hrs/day | 3 hrs/day | 4 hours/day |
| USE THE MOTIVATORS | 2 motivators only | 4 motivators | All motivators |

Remember that a plan is a living document, which needs changing to suit reality. If your initial estimates are wrong then change them. You may need 6 months to achieve these objectives if one particular activity delays you.

## We can do some things some of the times

As stated before, do not try to learn all the points and steps suggested in these chapters. It is much more important to understand the concepts and to know where to find the details when necessary.

For example, if you have to counsel someone tomorrow, then look up the section on counseling today to refresh your memory. You can do the same when you need to do some planning, training, discipline etc. You choose the things to do when you can control them. For example, there may be some activities that are more important to you that to other supervisors. In addition, there may be some improvements that are easy for you to achieve so why not do them earlier rather than later.

It is said that Einstein could not remember his home telephone number and when someone asked why not, he said, "why waste my brain cells on something that I can look up so easily"?

## We can do all things some of the times

This is the final stage where you consciously implement all the activities, at least once. With this experience you can continue to develop your management skills to the point when many will become second nature to you. There will always be times that you will need to refresh your memory on specific methods but this is the reason why you should make these chapters your best friend.

# Survival tips

## 1. Use the survival steps of the traffic lights

When you have a problem to resolve or a decision to make then ALWAYS do the following:

| **THE TRAFFIC LIGHTS** | |
|---|---|
| Red | Stop - Avoid an instant response |
| Orange | Think about it - Remember that there are nearly always alternatives. Although people will pressurize you for short-term instant attention they will always give more respect to well thought out solutions even if they have to wait a while. Time is the solution to so many problems. For example, give yourself time to refer to these notes as an aide to your thinking |
| Green | Respond positively - If you need more time then say so. Always make a decision even if the decision is to delay the final decision. At least you are taking the matter seriously with a positive response |

## 2. Find a champion (or champions)

Try to find or create a *champion,* someone who can support you and encourage you. The best person will always be your boss. Of course, you have to sell the idea to this person consciously in order to gain their support.

## 3. Do it as a group effort

This type of program is much more effective if ALL the supervisors are doing it together. Of course, if it is sponsored by the company then it's even better. Not only do you have a champion but also a support group.

## 3. Don't loose your sense of humor

Try to see the funny side of your inevitable failures. Laugh it off and start again.

That's it; there is no more to say because it is up to you now, to do it. I wish you all the luck that there is.

www.ingramcontent.com/pod-product-compliance
Ingram Content Group UK Ltd.
Pitfield, Milton Keynes, MK11 3LW, UK
UKHW021318180426
11947UKWH00015B/1303